MW01710750

LADY F

A British Lady across Patagonia

Six months' wanderings over unexplored and untrodden ground

EDICIONES HISTÓRICAS

Dixie, Florence
A British Lady Across Patagonia: Six months' wonderings over unexplored and untrodden ground / Florence Dixie. - 1ª ed. adaptada. - Ciudad Autónoma de Buenos Aires: Ediciones Históricas, 2023.
148 p.; 22 x 15 cm.

ISBN 978-987-48487-7-2

1. Crónica de Viajes. 2. Patagonia. I. Título.
CDD A863.

Published by Ediciones Históricas / Gerardo M. Bartolomé, established in Buenos Aires, Argentina.
For more information write to
Info@EdicionesHistoricas.com.ar or info@GerardoBartolome.com.

ISBN 978-987-48487-7-2

Cover by Gerardo Bartolomé.
Book design by Ricardo Dorr.

INDEX

TO

HIS ROYAL HIGHNESS,

ALBERT EDWARD, PRINCE OF WALES,

THIS WORK

DESCRIPTIVE OF

SIX MONTHS' WANDERINGS OVER UNEXPLORED

AND UNTRODDEN GROUND,

IS BY KIND PERMISSION RESPECTFULLY DEDICATED

BY HIS ROYAL HIGHNESS'S

OBLIGED AND OBEDIENT SERVANT,

THE AUTHOR.

INTRODUCTION BY THE PUBLISHER
Lady Florence Dixie (1855-1905)

Lady Florence Caroline Dixie (née Douglas) was no ordinary woman. "Of course,—somebody would say—she was a noble lady." But what made her an extraordinary woman was not her noble birth, quite the contrary. The despair that she felt because of her limited freedom, for being a woman, pushed her to break the model of a typical British Lady.

Florence Dixie was a feminist when the word "feminism" had not yet been invented.

It was her refusal to accept the life that the Victorian society had assigned to her that convinced her to seek adventure in an outlandish part of the world. When she read George Musters' book "At Home with the Patagonians" she understood that that was exactly the place she wanted to know. She convinced her husband and two of her brothers to escort her and so the small group left Great Britain in 1879 to sail towards the end of the world. Southern Patagonia was thought to be a dangerous land inhabited by tribes of giants, strange animals, limitless plains, snowy mountains and full of secrets to be discovered. This small group was leaded by a young woman, and so… a feminist was born.

Lady Florence's book, originally published as "Riding Across Patagonia", is not only about an untamed land but also about an untamed woman. Her description of this wild region also describes her desire to prove that women count, that women not only should be heard but can and should also be followed.

When Florence Dixie returned to Great Britain, she continued to persue a life completely different from others. Almost immediately she gained a commission as a war correspondent for The Morning Post to cover the Zulu Wars in South Africa and, upon her return, published "Land of Misfortune" (1882).

While from then on, all of her books always proposed the equality of sexes, it was in "Gloriana or the Revolution of 1900" (published in 1890) that she accomplished to condense the feminist spirit that would be a guiding light for many women at the end of the XIXth century. She not only predicted a fairer world for women, but she also started to pave the road in that direction.

Feminism was not her only quest. From her position she always sought to defend the rights of the weak such as that of the defeated Zulu King Cetswayo or her position for the Irish Home Rule, which earned her an assassination attempt in 1883 from which she escaped thanks to her dog. Also, a word must be said regarding her defence of the lives of animals. Even though in this book you'll read how thoughtlessly Lady Florence and her group hunted in Patagonia, she eventually changed her mind and started to argue against the hunting of wild animals (publishing "The Horrors of Sport" in 1891) and eventually became one of the founders of Vegetarianism in United Kingdom.

Lady Florence died of diphtheria in 1905, at the age of fifty and was buried in her family burial ground in Kinmount state, Scotland, in an unmarked spot, following her last wishes.

In EDICIONES HISTÓRICAS we've debated about changing the original name of her "Riding Across Patagonia" and came to the conclusion that since the book is much more than Patagonia we should move the focus of the title and publish it as "A British Lady Across Patagonia".

SCENE OF THE ATTACK

LADY FLORENCE DIXIE

THE WINDSOR ROAD, SHOWING THE WICKET GATE THROUGH WHICH HER LADYSHIP PASSED INTO THE PLANTATION WHERE SHE WAS ATTACKED

THE ST. BERNARD DOG, HUBERT, WHICH ATTACKED ONE OF HER LADYSHIP'S ASSAILANTS

"THE FISHERY," SIR BEAUMONT DIXIE'S WINDSOR RESIDENCE

THE ATTACK ON LADY FLORENCE DIXIE NEAR WINDSOR

CHAPTER I
Why Patagonia?

"Patagonia! who would ever think of going to such a place?" "Why, you will be eaten up by cannibals!" "What on earth makes you choose such an outlandish part of the world to go to?" "What can be the attraction?" "Why, it is thousands of miles away, and no one has ever been there before, except Captain Musters[1], and one or two other adventurous madmen!"

These, and similar questions and exclamations I heard from the lips of my friends and acquaintances, when I told them of my intended trip to Patagonia, the land of the Giants, the land of the fabled Golden City of Manoa. What was the attraction in going to an outlandish place so many miles away? The answer to the question was contained in its own words. Precisely because it was an outlandish place and so far away, I chose it. Palled for the moment with civilization and its surroundings, I wanted to escape somewhere, where I might be as far removed from them as possible. Many of my readers have doubtless felt the dissatisfaction with oneself, and everybody else, that comes over one at times in the midst of the pleasures of life; when one wearies of the shallow artificiality of modern existence; when what was once excitement has become so no longer, and a longing grows up within one to taste a more vigorous emotion than that afforded by the monotonous round of society's so-called "pleasures."

Well, it was in this state of mind that I cast round for some country which should possess the qualities necessary to satisfy my requirements, and finally I decided upon Patagonia as the most suitable. Without doubt there are wild countries more favoured by

---

1. George Musters, author of "At Home with the Patagonians" also published by Ediciones Históricas.

Nature in many ways. But nowhere else are you so completely alone. Nowhere else is there an area of 100,000 square miles which you may gallop over, and where, whilst enjoying a healthy, bracing climate, you are safe from the persecutions of fevers, friends, savage tribes, obnoxious animals, telegrams, letters, and every other nuisance you are elsewhere liable to be exposed to. To these attractions was added the thought, always alluring to an active mind, that there too I should be able to penetrate into vast wilds, virgin as yet to the foot of man. Scenes of infinite beauty and grandeur might be lying hidden in the silent solitude of the mountains which bound the barren plains of the Pampas, into whose mysterious recesses no one as yet had ever ventured. And I was to be the first to behold them! An egotistical pleasure, it is true; but the idea had a great charm for me, as it has had for many others. Thus, under the combined influence of the above considerations, it was decided that Patagonia was to be the chosen field of my new experiences.

My party consisted of Lord Queensberry and Lord James Douglas, my two brothers, my husband, and myself, and a friend, Mr. J. Beerbohm, whose book, Wanderings in Patagonia, had just been published when we left England. We only took one servant with us, knowing that English servants inevitably prove a nuisance and hindrance in expeditions of the kind, when a great deal of "roughing it" has to be gone through, as they have an unpleasant knack of falling ill at inopportune moments.

Our outfit was soon completed, and shipped, together with our other luggage, on board the good ship "Britannia," which sailed from Liverpool on the 11th of December 1878. We ourselves were going overland to join her at Bordeaux, as we thereby had a day longer in England. Then came an unpleasant duty, taking leave of our friends. I hate saying good-bye. On the eve of a long journey, one cannot help thinking of the uncertainty of everything in this world. The voice that bids you God-speed may, before you return, perhaps be silent for ever. The face of each friend who grasps your hand vividly recalls some scene of pleasant memory. Now it reminds you of some hot August day among the purple hills of Scotland, when a good bag, before an excellent lunch, had been followed by some more than usually exciting sport. The Highlands had never looked so beautiful, so merry a party had never clambered down the moors homeward, so successful a day had never been followed by so jolly an evening;

and then, with a sigh, as your friend leaves you, you ask yourself, "Shall I ever climb the moors again?" Now it is to Leicestershire that your memory reverts. The merry blast of the huntsman's horn resounds, the view-halloa rings out cheerily on the bright crisp air of a fine hunting morning; the fox is "gone away," you have got a good start, and your friend has too. "Come on," he shouts, "let us see this run together!" Side by side you fly the first fence, take your horse in hand, and settle down to ride over the broad grass country. How distinctly you remember that run, how easily you recall each fence you flew together, each timber-rail you topped, and that untempting bottom you both got so luckily and safely over, and above all, the old farmyard, where the gallant fox yielded up his life. Meanwhile, with a forced smile and a common-place remark, you part; and together, perhaps, you may never hear the huntsman's horn, never charge the ox-fence, never strive to be foremost in the chase again!

With these thoughts passing through my mind I began to wonder why I wanted to leave England. I remembered for the moment only the pleasant features of the past, and remembering them, forgot the feelings and circumstances which had prompted me to embark on my present enterprise. The stern sex will possibly reprehend this exhibition of female fickleness of purpose. May I urge in its palliation that my weakness scarcely lasted longer than it has taken me to write this?

14th December.—On a cold, rainy afternoon we steamed down from Bordeaux in a little tender to join the "Britannia," which was anchored off Pauillac. We were soon alongside, and were welcomed on board by Captain Brough, under whose guidance we inspected, with a good deal of interest, the fine ship which was to be our home for some time. It would be superfluous for me to describe the excellent internal arrangements on board; few of my readers, I imagine, but are acquainted, either from experience or description, with the sumptuous and comfortable fittings-up of an Ocean passenger-steamer.

Soon the anchor was up—the propeller was in motion, and our nerves had hardly recovered from the shock inflicted by the report of the gun which fired the parting salute, ere Pauillac was scarcely distinguishable in the mist and rain astern. By the time dinner was over we were altogether out of sight of land, the rain was still falling heavily, and prognostications of dirty weather were being indulged in by the sailors. Giving a last look at the night, I turned into the captain's cosy deck-house, where I found my companions deep in the intricacies and wranglings of a rubber at whist, in which I, too, presently took a hand. As time went on, indications that it was getting rather rough were not wanting, in the swaying of the ship and the noise of the wind; but so comfortable were we in our little cabin, with the curtains drawn and lamps lit, that we were quite astonished when the captain paid us a visit at about nine o'clock and told us that it was blowing a regular gale.

The words were hardly out of his mouth when the ship heeled suddenly over under a tremendous shock, which was followed by a mighty rush of water along the decks. We ran out, thinking we must have struck a rock. The night was as black as pitch, and the roaring of the wind, the shouts of the sailors, and the wash of the water along the decks, heightened with their deafening noise, the anxiety of the moment. Fortunately, the shock we had experienced had no worse cause than an enormous sea, which had struck the ship forward, and swept right aft, smashing whatever opposed its destructive course, and bending thick iron stanchions as if they had been mere wires.

As soon as the hubbub attendant on this incident had somewhat subsided, thankful that it had been no worse, we returned to our game at whist, which occupied us till eleven o'clock, at which hour, "all lights out" being the order of the ship, we turned into our cabins to sleep the first night of many on board the "Britannia."

The next day was fine and sunny, and so the weather continued till we reached Lisbon, three days after leaving Bordeaux, when it grew rather rough again. At Lisbon we remained a day, taking in coal and fresh provisions—and then once more weighed anchor, not to drop it again till the shores of the New World should have been reached.

Just as it was beginning to dawn on the morning of the second day after leaving Lisbon, I was awakened by the speed of the vessel being reduced to half its usual ratio, for so accustomed does one become in a short time to the vibration of the screw, that any change from its ordinary force immediately disturbs one's sleep. Looking out of my cabin-window I could see that we were close to land, so, dressing hurriedly, I went on deck. We seemed to be but a stone's-throw from an island, whose bold rugged heights rose up darkly against the pale light that shone in the morning sky. At one point of the shore the revolving light of a beacon flashed redly at intervals, growing fainter and fainter each time, as day slowly broke, and a golden haze began to flood the eastern horizon. In the darkness the island looked like a huge bare rock, but daylight showed it clothed in tolerably luxuriant vegetation. The presence of man was indicated by the little white houses, which could be distinguished nestling in crannies of its apparently steep green slopes. This was the island of Palma, one of the Canary group, and small though it looked, it numbers a good many inhabitants, and furnishes a fair contingent of emigrants to the River Plate, where "Canarios," as they are called, are favourably looked upon, being a skilful, industrious race.

The days slipped quickly by, and soon, as we neared the equator, it began to grow intensely hot. Christmas Day spent in the tropics did not rightly appear as such, though we kept it in the orthodox manner, the head-steward preparing quite a banquet, at which much merriment reigned, and many speeches were spoken.

We arrived at Pernambuco on the 28th of December, but did not go on shore, as we were only stopping in the port a couple of hours, and were told, moreover, that there is nothing to be seen when one is there. We amused ourselves watching the arrival of some fresh Brazilian passengers, who were going with us to Rio. The extensiveness of their get-up might have vied with that of Solomon "in all his glory"—but tall hats, white trousers, and frock-coats seemed ludicrously out of place on board ship. Not less funny was the effusiveness of their affectionate leave-takings. At parting they clasped their friends to their breasts, interchanging kisses in the most pathetic manner, and evincing an absence of *mauvaise honte* in the presence of us bystanders, which was at once edifying and refreshing. *Autres pays, autres mœurs.*

Some boatmen came alongside, bringing baskets of the celebrated Pernambuco white pineapples. We bought some of this fruit, which we thought delicious: it is the only tropical fruit which, in my opinion, can vie with European kinds. "Luscious tropical fruit" sounds very well, as does "the flashing Southern Cross;" but nearer acquaintance with both proves very disappointing and dispels any of the illusions one may have acquired respecting them, from the over-enthusiastic descriptions of imaginative travellers. Very soon the captain came offshore again, with the mails, etc. A bell was rung, the fruit-vendors were bundled over the side of the ship, chattering and vociferating,—last kisses were interchanged by the Brazilian passengers and their friends, up went the anchor, round went the screw, bang! went our parting salute, and, thank God, we are off again, with a slight breeze stealing coolingly over us, doubly grateful after the stifling heat which oppressed us while at anchor.

CHAPTER II
Brazil

A day after leaving Pernambuco we dropped anchor again; this time in the magnificent "Bahia de todos os Santos," the ample dimensions of which make its name a not inapposite one. Bahia itself is built on a high ridge of land, which runs out into the sea, and forms a point at the entrance of the harbour. The town is half hidden among huge banana trees and coconut palms and seen from on board looks picturesque enough. After breakfast our party went on shore, accompanied by the captain, and for an hour or so we walked about the streets and markets of the lower town, which stands at the base of the ridge above mentioned. We found it as dirty and ugly as could well be, and our sense of smell had no little violence done to it by the disagreeable odours which pervaded the air. There was a great deal of movement going on everywhere, and the streets swarmed with black slaves, male and female, carrying heavy loads of salt meat, sacks of rice, and other merchandise to and from the warehouses which lined the quays. They all seemed to be very happy, to judge by their incessant chatter and laughter, and not overworked either, I should think, for they were most of them plump enough, the women especially being many of them almost inconveniently fat. Finding little to detain us in the lower town, we had ourselves transported to the upper in an hydraulic lift, which makes journeys up and down every five minutes.

Then we got into a mule-tramway, which bowled us along the narrow streets at a famous pace. Soon getting clear of the dirty town, we drove along a pleasant high-road, on either side of which stood pretty little villas, shaded by palms and banana-trees, and encircled by trim well-kept gardens, bright with a profusion of tropical flowers. Now and then we could catch a glimpse of the sea too, and as we went along we found the tram was taking us out to the extreme point of the ridge mentioned above. Before we reached it we had to change our conveyance once or twice, as occasionally we came to a descent so steep that carriages worked up and down by hydraulic machinery had been established to ply in conjunction with the ordinary mule-trams. At last we were set down close to the seashore, near a lighthouse which stands in a commanding position on the point. The view which was now before us was a splendid one; the immense bay lay at our feet, and beyond spread the ocean, dotted with the tiny white sails of numberless catamarans, as the queer native fishing-boats are called, which looked like white gulls resting on its blue waters. But the heat in the open was so overpowering that we soon had to take refuge in a little *café* close by, where we had some luncheon, after which we went back to Bahia the way we had come, by no means sorry to get on board the cool, clean ship again. Half an hour after our arrival the anchor was weighed, and we steamed off, *en route* for Rio de Janeiro.

New Year's Day, like Christmas Day, was passed at sea, and we celebrated it with much festivity. Altogether our life on board was a most agreeable one, thanks to the kindness and attentions of the captain and his officers, and the days flew by with surprising rapidity. Four days after leaving Bahia we sighted land off Rio, at an early hour of the morning. Anxious to lose nothing of the scenery, I had risen at about four o'clock, and certainly I had no reason to repent of my eagerness. We had passed Cape Frio, and were steaming along a line of coast which runs from the cape up to the opening of the bay. Thick mists hung over the high peaks and hills, shrouding their outlines, and along the shore the surf broke with a sullen roar against the base of the cliffs which fell abruptly down to the sea. As yet all was grey and indistinct. But presently the sun, which for a long time had been struggling with the mists, shone victoriously forth; the fog disappeared as if by magic, disclosing, bathed in the glow of sunrise, a grand scene of palm-covered cliffs and mountains, which rose, range beyond range, as far as the eye could reach. In front of us lay Rio Harbour, with the huge Pão de Açucar, or Sugar Loaf Mountain, standing like a gigantic sentry at its entrance. In shape it is exactly like the article of grocery from which it takes its name, and rises abruptly, a solid mass of smooth rock, to a height of 1270 feet. Its summit, long considered inaccessible, was reached by some English middies a few years ago. Much to the anger and disgust of

Rio de Janeiro in 1870,
by Nicola Facchinetti

the inhabitants of Rio, these adventurous youngsters planted the Union Jack on the highest point of the Loaf, and there it floated, no one daring to go up to take it down, till a patriotic breeze swept it away. Directly opposite is the Fort Santa Cruz, which, with its 120 guns, forms the principal defence of the harbour. Soon we were gliding past it and threading our way through the numerous craft which studded the bay, we presently dropped anchor in front of Rio, and found ourselves at leisure to examine the harbour, one of the finest and largest in the world. Covering a space of sixteen miles in a north and south direction, it gradually widens from about three-quarters of a mile at its entrance to fifteen miles at its head. The town stands on the western side of the bay, at about two miles from its entrance. It is backed by a high range of mountains, and, as seen from the bay, nestling amidst oceans of green, presents a most pleasing appearance. The harbour is dotted with little islands, and all along its shores are scattered villages, country seats, and plantations.

As soon as the captain had got through his duties, we took our places in his boat, and started off for the shore. On landing at a slippery, dirty, stone causeway, we were surrounded by a crowd of negroes, who jabbered and grinned and gesticulated like so many monkeys.

Making our way through their midst, we passed by the marketplace, and then, threading a number of hot, dirty, little streets, we at last got into the main street of the town, which was rather broad, and shaded on either side by a row of trees.

The public buildings at Rio are all distinguished by their peculiar ugliness. They are mostly painted yellow, a hue which seems to prevail everywhere here, possibly in order to harmonise with the complexion of the inhabitants. The cathedral forms no exception to the general rule. We entered it for a moment, thinking that we might possibly see some good pictures from the time of the Portuguese dominion. But we found everything covered up in brown holland. Nossa Senhora da Francisca, or whatever virgin saint the church is dedicated to, was evidently in curl-papers, and we could see nothing, though we could smell a great deal more than was agreeable. Truly I did not envy the saints their odour of sanctity. To my mundane nostrils this same odour smacked strongly of garlic and other abominations. We soon got tired of wandering aimlessly about and feeling little desire to stop in the town any longer, we hired a carriage and started off for a little place called Tijuca, which lies high up among the hills behind Rio.

Our coach was drawn by four fine mules, who galloped along the streets at a rattling and—inasmuch as the driver was evidently an unskilful one—an undesirable pace. We remonstrated with him, but were told that it was the custom of the country to drive at that rate. So, in deference to the "custom of the country," on we went at full gallop, shaving lamp-posts, twisting round sharp corners, frightening foot-passengers, and narrowly missing upsetting, or being upset by, other vehicles which came in the way.

I was quite thankful when we at last got safely clear of the town. The road lay amongst the most beautiful scenery, and the heat, though considerable, was not oppressive enough to interfere with my enjoyment of it. After a couple of hours' driving we halted to give the mules a rest near a little brook, which came rippling out from the shady mass of vegetation which lined the road. I sat down under a banana tree, letting my eyes wander in lazy admiration over the scene at our feet. We had gradually got to a good height above Rio, and through a frame of leaves and flowers I could see the town, the blue bay studded with tiny green islands, and beyond, the rugged mountains, with a light mist hanging like a silver veil over their purple slopes.

When the mules were sufficiently rested we got into the carriage, and starting at a brisk trot, it was not long before we got to the summit of a hill, at the foot of which, in a little valley, lies Tijuca. Before reaching it a rather stiff incline had to be descended, and one of the wheelers, either blown or obstinate, refused to hold the carriage back. The driver insisted that the animal was only showing temper, and commenced to flog it. Foreseeing the result, we all got out of the carriage, and left the man to his own devices. He persisted in whipping the recalcitrant mule, and, as might have been expected, he presently started the other animals off at full gallop, leaving their comrade the option of following suit or falling. It chose the latter course, and after a good deal of slipping and sliding, went down with a tremendous crash. The other three, taking fright, immediately bolted, and we soon lost sight of carriage and driver in a cloud of dust. We followed on down the hill as fast as we could, rather anxious for the safety of the driver. Here and there, as we hurried along, we came across a piece of broken harness, and presently, on turning a sharp corner, we suddenly came upon the overturned carriage, the mules struggling and kicking in a confused heap, and the driver, unhurt but frightened, sitting in the grass by the side of the road. Assistance having been procured from Tijuca, which was close at hand, the mules were freed, and the carriage raised off the dragged mule, which we expected to find killed. To our surprise, however, no sooner were its limbs at liberty than it sprang up and began to crop the grass in utter unconcern as to the numerous wounds all over its body. A horse in such a state would have been completely cowed, and would probably never have been of any use again.

Leaving the driver to make the best of his position, we walked down to the Hotel Whyte, which lies snugly ensconced among palms and orange-groves at Tijuca. The building, with its clean cool rooms, shaded by verandas, looked particularly inviting after the establishments we had been in at Rio, and it was pleasant too, to be waited on by Englishmen—the proprietor and his staff being of that nationality. A little stream runs past the hotel, feeding a basin which has been hewn out of the rock, where visitors can refresh themselves with a plunge, a privilege of which the gentlemen of our party were not slow to profit.

After I had rested a little, I strolled away among the woods, feasting my eyes on the beauty and novelty of the vegetation, and on the delightful glimpses of scenery I occasionally stumbled across, to attempt to describe which would only be doing them an injustice. But that even this paradise had its drawbacks I was not long in discovering. I was about to throw myself on a soft green bank, fringed with gold and silver ferns and scarlet begonias, that stretched along a sparkling rivulet, when suddenly my little terrier darted at something that was lying on the bank, and pursued it for a second, till my call brought her back. The "something" was a snake of the Cross, whose bite is almost instantaneously fatal, and as I quickly retraced my steps to safer ground I thanked my stars that I had been spared a closer acquaintance with this deadly reptile. When I got back I had a swim in the rocky basin above mentioned, which refreshed me wonderfully. Soon afterwards we sat down to dinner, winding up the day by a cheery musical evening.

Before going to bed, enticed by the beauty of the night, I strolled for an hour or more among the woods at the back of the hotel, and gradually, attracted by the noise of falling waters, I made my way to a little cataract, which, coming from some rocky heights above, dashed foaming into a broad basin, and swirling and bubbling over a stony bed, disappeared below in the shadows of a lonely glen. The moon, which was now shining brightly, cast a pale gleam over its waters, and myriads of fireflies flashed around like showers of sparks. Not a sound was heard save the roar of the water, and hardly a breath of wind stirred the giant foliage of the sleeping forests. For a long time I sat giving myself up to the softening influences of my surroundings, and thinking, amidst the splendour of that warm tropical night, of the dear old country far away, now, no doubt, covered with ice and snow.

As we had to be on board the steamer by twelve o'clock the next morning, the carriages were ordered for eight o'clock, by which time we were up and had breakfasted. The captain, my husband, brother, and myself, took our seats in a carriage drawn by two mules, Queensberry and Mr. B. following in a Victoria. Having said good-bye to Mr. Whyte, we told our driver to start, cautioning him, as he was the same Jehu who had driven us so recklessly the day before, to be more careful. But again, for some unaccountable reason, he cracked his whip and started off at full gallop. Again, the mules bolted, and like lightning we went down a little incline which leads from the hotel to the road. Then a sharp turn had to be made, seeing which we held on like grim death to the carriage, an upset being now palpably inevitable. On we went—the carriage heeled over, balanced itself for a moment on its two left wheels, and then, catching the corner of a stone bridge, over it went with a crash, burying us four luckless occupants beneath it, and hurling the driver into the brook below. Happily the shock had thrown the mules as well, for had they galloped on, huddled as we were pell-mell among the wheels of the carriage, the accident must have ended in some disaster. As it was, we had a most miraculous escape. The driver, who meanwhile had picked himself, drenched and crestfallen, out of the brook, came in for a shower of imprecations, which his stupidity and recklessness had well-earned for him. He made some feeble attempts at an explanation, but no one understood him, and he only aggravated the virulence of our righteous wrath.

However, something had to be done, and quickly, if we were to reach the steamer by twelve o'clock. The Victoria was now the only conveyance left, and we could not all get into it. As luck would have it, whilst we were debating, a diligence was seen coming along the road, and, as it proved, there were sufficient vacant seats to accommodate all our party,—Queensberry, Mr. B. and myself going in the Victoria. The driver having assured us that the mules were perfectly quiet, and he himself appearing a steadier sort of man than the other unfortunate creature, we felt more at ease, and certainly at first start all went smoothly enough. But, strange to say, we were doomed to incur a third upset. When we came to a steep descent, instead of driving slowly, our coachman, for some inexplicable reason, actually urged his animals into a gallop. We called to him to stop, but that was already beyond his power, the mules having again bolted, and, to make matters still more desperate, one of the reins broke, leaving us completely at the mercy of accidents. The road wound down the side of a steep hill, and each time the swaying carriage swung round one of the sharp curves we were in imminent danger of being dashed over the roadside, down a precipice three hundred feet in depth. The peril of this eventuality increased with our momentum, and, as the lesser of two evils, we had to choose jumping out of the carriage. This we did at a convenient spot, and fortunately, though we were all severely cut and bruised, no bones were broken. In another second the coach and driver would have disappeared over the precipice had not one of the mules suddenly fallen, and acting as a drag on the coach, enabled the driver to check the other mule just in the nick of time.

To meet with three accidents in twenty-four hours was rather too much of a good thing and vowing that we had had enough of Brazilian coachmanship to last us all our lives, we completed the rest of the way on foot, arriving two hours after the appointed time, on board the old "Britannia." We presented a very strange appearance, our clothes torn and dust-stained, and our faces covered with cuts and bruises; but a bath and a little court-plaster soon put us all right, and we were on deck again in time to have a last look at Rio as we steamed away.

CHAPTER III
Patagonia at Last

I could not repress a pang of regret as we steamed slowly out of Rio Harbour. There may be scenes more impressively sublime; there are, without doubt, landscapes fashioned on a more gigantic scale; by the side of the Himalayas or the Alps, the mountains around Rio are insignificant enough, and one need not go out of England in search for charming and romantic scenery. But nowhere have the rugged and the tender, the wild and the soft, been blended into such exquisite *union* as at Rio, and it is this quality of unrivalled contrasts, that, to my mind, gives to that scenery its charm of unsurpassed loveliness. Nowhere else is there such audacity, such fierceness even of outline, coupled with such multiform splendour of colour, such fairy-like delicacy of detail. As a precious jewel is encrusted by the coarse rock, the smiling bay lies encircled by frowning mountains of colossal proportions and the most capricious shapes. In the production of this work the most opposite powers of nature have been laid under contribution. The awful work of the volcano; the immense boulders of rock which lie piled up to the clouds in irregular masses, have been clothed in a brilliant web of tropical vegetation, spun from sunshine and mist. Here nature revels in manifold creation, life multiplies itself a million-fold, the soil bursts with exuberance of fertility, and the profusion of vegetable and animal life beggars description. Every tree is clothed with a thousand luxuriant creepers, purple and scarlet-blossomed; they in their turn support myriads of lichens and other verdant parasites. The plants shoot up with marvellous rapidity, and glitter with flowers of the rarest hues and shapes, or bear quantities of luscious fruit, pleasant to the eye and sweet to the taste. The air resounds with the hum of insect-life; through the bright green leaves of the banana skim the sparkling hummingbirds, and gorgeous butterflies of enormous size float, glowing with every colour of the rainbow on the flower-scented breezes. But over all this beauty, over the luxuriance of vegetation, over the softness of the tropical air, over the splendour of the sunshine, over the perfume of the flowers, Pestilence has cast her fatal miasmas, and, like the sword of Damocles, the yellow fever hangs threateningly over the head of those who dwell among these lovely scenes. Nature, however, is not to be blamed for this drawback to one of her most charming creations. With better drainage and cleanlier habits amongst its population, there is no reason why Rio should not be a perfectly healthy place. To exorcise the demon who annually scourges its people, no acquaintance with the black art is necessary. The scrubbing-brush and Windsor soap—"this only is the witchcraft need be used." Four days after leaving Rio we arrived at Monte Video[1], but as we came from an infected port we were put into quarantine, much to our disgust, and were of course unable to go on shore. After we had discharged what cargo we carried for Monte Video, we proceeded to a little island, where we were to land the quarantine passengers, amongst whom was my brother Queensberry, who wanted to stop in Monte Video for a fortnight, following us by the next steamer. The quarantine island, which was a bare rocky little place, did not look at all inviting, and I certainly did not envy my brother his three-days' stay on it. He told me afterwards that he had never passed such a miserable time in all his life, the internal domestic arrangements being most primitive.

The days after leaving Monte Video passed swiftly enough, as it had got comparatively cool, and we were able to have all kinds of games on deck. After seven days at sea, early one morning we sighted Cape Virgins, which commands the north-eastern entrance to the Straits of Magellan. The south-eastern point is called Cape Espiritu Santo; the distance between the two capes being about twenty-two miles. Whilst we were threading the intricate passage of the First Narrows, which are not more than two miles broad, I scanned with interest the land I had come so many thousand miles to see—Patagonia at last! Desolate and dreary enough it looked, a succession of bare plateaus, not a tree nor a shrub visible anywhere; a grey, shadowy country, which seemed hardly of this world; such a landscape,

1. Although many travellers refer to this city as Monte Video, the true spelling was and is today Montevideo.

in fact, as one might expect to find on reaching some other planet. Much as I had been astonished by the glow and exuberance of tropical life at Rio, the impression it had made on my mind had to yield in intensity to the vague feelings of awe and wonder produced by the sight of the huge barren solitudes now before me.

After passing the Second Narrows, Elizabeth Island, so named by Sir Francis Drake, came in sight. Its shores were covered with wild fowl and seabirds, chiefly shag. Flocks of these birds kept flying round the ship, and the water itself, through which we passed, literally teemed with gulls and every imaginable kind of sea-fowl. We were soon abreast of Cape Negro, about fourteen miles from Sandy Point[2]. Here the character of the country suddenly changes, for Cape Negro is the point of the last southerly spur of the Cordilleras, which runs along the coast, joining the main ridge beyond Sandy Point. All these spurs, like the Cordilleras themselves, are clothed with beech forests and thick underwood of the magnolia species, a vegetation, however, which ends as abruptly as the spurs, from the thickly-wooded sides of which, to the completely bare plains, there is no graduation whatever.

As we went along, we passed a couple of canoes containing Fuegians, the inhabitants of the Tierra del Fuego, but they were too far off to enable me to judge of their appearance, though I should have liked to have had a good look at them. They are reputed to be cannibals, and no doubt justly so. I have even been told that in winter, when other food is scarce, they kill off their own old men and women, though of course they prefer a white man if obtainable.

At one o'clock we cast anchor off Sandy Point. This settlement is called officially by the Chileans, to whom it belongs, "La Colonia de Magallanes." It was formerly only a penal colony, but in consequence of the great increase of traffic through the Straits, the attention of the Chilean Government was drawn to the importance the place might ultimately assume, and, accordingly, grants of land and other inducements were offered to emigrants. But the colony up to the present has never flourished as was expected, and during a mutiny

2. The city's name of Punta Arenas has its origin on Parker-King's expedition in 1826-1830 who named the place (in English) after the "sandy point", or more precisely, the small sandy peninsula, that can still be seen today not far from the harbour.

Sandy Point or Punta Arenas
by Robert Cunningham

which took place there in 1877, many of the houses were burned down, and a great deal of property destroyed. As the steamer was to leave in two hours, we began preparations for landing, but meantime the breeze, which had sprung up shortly after our arrival, freshened into a gale, and the sea grew so rough that it was impossible to lower a boat, and the lighters that had come offshore to fetch away cargo dared not go back. The gale lasted all day and the greater part of the night, calming down a little towards three o'clock in the morning. Every effort was accordingly made to get us on shore, the alternative being that we should have to go on with the steamer to Valparaiso, the Company's regulations not allowing more than a certain length of time to be spent at Sandy Point. As may be imagined, we by no means liked the idea of such a possible consummation, and the weather was eagerly scanned, whilst our luggage and traps were being hurried over the sides, as a fresh increase in the strength of the wind would have been fatal.

At last, all was ready; we said good-bye to the captain and officers, to whose kindness during the voyage we were so much indebted for our enjoyment of our trip on board the "Britannia"—and climbing down the gangway took our seats in the boat which was to carry us ashore. I felt quite sad as we rowed away, leaving behind us the good ship which we had come to look upon as a home, and for which I at least felt almost a personal affection.

After a long pull, during which the contrary wind and tide bade fair to set at nought the efforts of the four strong sailors who rowed us ashore, we at last came alongside the old tumble-down wooden pier, which forms the landing stage at Sandy Point. We succeeded in reaching its end without incurring any mishap, though we ran considerable risk from the many dangers with which it bristled, in the shape of sudden yawning holes, and treacherously shifting planks. This pier, however, had the merit—a questionable one it is true—of being in keeping with the appearance and condition of the whole colony to which it served as a warning introduction. I suppose there possibly may be drearier looking places than the town of Sandy Point, but I do not think it is probable; and as we walked over the sand-covered beach in front of the settlement, and surveyed the gloomy rows of miserable wooden huts, the silent, solitary streets, where, at that moment, not a single living being was to be seen, save some hungry-looking ostrich-hound, we all agreed that the epithet of "God-forsaken hole" was the only description that did justice to the merits of this desolate place,—nor did subsequent and fuller acquaintance with it by any means induce us to alter this unfavourable opinion.

Proceeding under the guidance of Mr. Dunsmuir, the English Consul, we halted about two hundred yards from the pier, at a house which, we were informed, was the principal shop and inn in the place. It was not an ambitious establishment. Its interior consisted of a ground-floor containing two rooms, of which one served as a shop, and the other as a sitting room. This last apartment we secured as a storeroom for our luggage and equipment, and there also we ate our meals during our sojourn in Sandy Point. The upper portion of this magnificent dwelling was a kind of loft, in one corner of which was a small compartment, which my brother and Mr. B. used as a bedroom. Through the kindness of Mr. Dunsmuir my husband and myself were lodged very comfortably in his own house.

Our first experience of "roughing it," in the shape of the breakfast with which Pedro the innkeeper supplied us, being over, we sauntered up through the grass-grown streets of the colony to the house of Mr. Dunsmuir, from which, as it stands on high ground, we obtained a good view of the Straits and the opposite shores of the Tierra del Fuego. The "Britannia" had already weighed anchor, and for a long time we watched her steaming away through the Straits, till, growing gradually smaller and smaller, she at last disappeared in the haze of the distant horizon. And now that the last link, as it were, of the chain which bound me to old England was gone, for the first time I began to fully *realise* the fact that we were ten thousand miles away from our home and our friends, alone amidst strange faces and wild scenes; and it required almost an effort to banish the impression that the whole thing was a dream, from which I was presently to awaken and find myself back in England again.

Our anxiety to leave Sandy Point as soon as possible hastened preparations we had to make before starting; but even with every wish to get away, there was so much to be done that we calculated we should not be ready to start for at least four days. There were guides to be found, good dogs to be bought, and, above all, suitable horses to be hired or purchased. Numbers of these latter animals were brought for our inspection, from among which we selected about fifty, of whose merits and failings I shall have to speak at a later occasion. We found the charges for everything ridiculously high, and though no doubt we were cheated on all sides, there was nothing to be done but to accept the prices and conditions demanded, as guides were not plentiful, and the other necessities procurable nowhere else.

A whole day was spent in unpacking the provisions and equipment we had brought from England, and in putting them into canvas bags, so as to be conveniently portable on horseback. For the benefit of those who may contemplate an expedition similar to ours, I give the following list of the articles and provisions we took with us. We limited ourselves, I may say *en passant*, to such things as were absolutely indispensable, the disadvantages arising from being burdened with unnecessary luggage on such a trip being self-evident:—Two small tents (*tentes d'abri*), 2 hatchets, 1 pail, 1 iron pot for cooking, 1 frying-pan, 1 saucepan, biscuits, coffee, tea, sugar, flour, oatmeal, preserved milk, and a few tins of butter, 2 kegs of whisky.

To the above we added a sack of *yerba mate*[3], of which herb we all grew so fond that we ultimately used it to the complete exclusion

3. Yerba mate or simply "mate" is a kind of green tea very popular in Argentina, Uruguay, southern Brazil and (surprisingly) southern Chile. The "yerba" or grass, comes northern Argentina and southern Brazil, as was historically cultivated by the Guarani tribes.

of tea and coffee, although at first, we by no means agreed with the enthusiastic description of its merits given by Mr. B., at whose recommendation we had taken it.

Our personal outfit consisted, in addition to a few changes of woollen underclothing, in a guanaco-fur mantle, a rug or two, a sheath-knife and revolver; besides, of course, the guns and rifles we had brought for sporting purposes. The cartridges for the latter, of which we had a great number, formed the heaviest item of weight; but notwithstanding the care we had used in our calculations, so as not to take more provisions than we wanted, the goodly pile which was formed when all our luggage was heaped together was rather alarming, and we found that twelve horses at least would be required to carry it. Fortunately, we were able to procure three mules, who, between them, carried more than six horses could have done, without, moreover, suffering half as much as the latter in condition from fatigue, or the severe heat which we occasionally encountered.

We selected our guides from among a number who offered their services. We chose four; two Frenchmen, an Argentine gaucho, and a nondescript creature, an inhabitant of Sandy Point, I'Aria[4] by name, who had accompanied Captain Musters on his expedition. This I'Aria was a dried-up-looking being of over sixty, but he proved a useful servant, notwithstanding his age. He was a beautiful rider; and, considering his years, wonderfully active and enduring. As long as we remained in Sandy Point, however, he was of little use to us, as he was never by any chance sober, though, strange to say, when once we left the settlement, he became a total abstainer, and stoutly refused, during the whole of the trip, to take any liquor that was offered to him. His face, the skin of which, from long exposure to wind and weather, had acquired the consistency of parchment, was one mass of wrinkles, and burnt almost black by the sun, while the watchful, cunning expression of his twinkling bead-like eyes added to his wild appearance, the Mephistophelian character of which earned for him the sobriquet of "The devil's agent for Patagonia." He had passed more than forty years of his life on the pampa, and was, therefore, well qualified to act as guide. Of the others, Gregorio gave us most satisfaction, and served us all through the trip with untiring zeal and

4. The person's name, according to Musters, was Jaria but we decided to leave Lady Florence's spelling.

fidelity. He was a good-looking man, of about forty, and added to the other accomplishments of his craft as gaucho, a slight knowledge of English. His ordinary occupation was that of an Indian trader, and at one time of his career he had owned a small schooner, with which he used to go seal-hunting in the season. One of the Frenchmen, François, whose original profession had been that of a cook, proved most useful to us in that capacity, and played the changes on what would otherwise have been a slightly monotonous diet of guanaco and ostrich meat, in a marvellous manner. His career, like Gregorio's, had been a chequered one. After having served during the Franco-Prussian war as a Chasseur d'Afrique, he left his country with three companions to start some business in South America, on the failure of which he turned his attention to ostrich-hunting. He was a cheery, handsome little fellow, and was possessed, moreover, of an excellent voice, and whether at work by the campfire, or riding on the march, was always to be heard singing merrily. He owned two very good ostrich-dogs; one, a handsome Scotch deer hound called "Leona[5]" the other a black wiry dog called "Loca[6]" a cross between an African greyhound and an English lurcher. Gregorio had only one dog, but it was the best of the lot, often managing to run down an ostrich singly, a feat which requires immense stamina and gameness, and which none of the other dogs were able to perform.

As to Guillaume I need say nothing, except that all our party disliked him very much.

After four days' hard work our preparations for departure were nearly completed, though a little yet remained to be done. Anxious, however, to get out of Sandy Point, we resolved to start off with the greater part of the packs and horses, and to await the coming of the remainder in the beech-wood at Cabo Negro, some fifteen miles away from the colony.

---

5. Lioness.

6. Crazy.

CHAPTER IV
Riding along the Straits

Early in the morning the horses were driven up and saddled, some trouble being experienced with the pack-mules, who were slightly restive, taking rather unkindly to their loads at first.

As our guides were busy hunting up the requisite number of horses, and finishing their preparations for the journey, we took another man with us for the time that we should have to remain at Cabo Negro, as well as a little boy, a son of Gregorio's, to help to drive the horses along. After a hurried breakfast we got into the saddle; the pack-horses were driven together, not without a great deal of trouble, for they were as yet strangers to each other, and every now and then one or two would bolt off, a signal to the whole troop to disperse all over the place, so that nearly an hour had elapsed before we had got well clear of the colony, and found ourselves riding over an undulating grassy stretch, *en route* for the pampas.

The Straits of Magellan

Our way lay over this plain for about an hour, and then, having forded a small stream, we entered the outskirts of the beechwood forests that line the Straits. The foliage of the trees was fresh and green, the sky clear and blue, the air sun-lit and buoyant, and everything seeming to augur favourably for the success of our trip, we were all in the best of spirits.

Our road presently brought us down to the Straits of Magellan, along whose narrow strip of beach, in some places barely three yards broad, we had now to ride in single file. Along the coast the land terminates abruptly, and the trees and bushes form an impenetrable thicket, which comes down almost to the water's edge. Point after point shoots out into the sea, each bearing a monotonous resemblance to the other, though, as we advanced, the vegetation that covered them grew more and more stunted and scanty, till at last the trees and bushes disappeared altogether, and after a three hours' ride we found ourselves journeying along under the shadow of some steep bluffs, on which the only vegetation was a profusion of long coarse grass. Innumerable species of gulls and albatrosses were disporting themselves on the blue water, and seemed little alarmed at our approach, lazily rising from the water a moment as we went past them, to resume almost immediately their fishing operations. All along the beach, carried there by the sea from the opposite side, I noticed great quantities of the cooked shells of crayfish, the remains of many a Fuegian-Indian meal. The Tierra del Fuego itself was distinctly visible opposite, and at different points we could see tall columns of smoke rising up into the still air, denoting the presence of native encampments, just as Magellan had seen them four hundred years before, giving to the island, on that account, the name it still bears.

At Cabo Negro we stopped for a moment at a little farmhouse, and partook of some mate, which was hospitably offered us by the farmer's wife, and then mounting again, we galloped over a broad grassy plain where some sheep and cattle were grazing, till we came to a steep, wooded hill. On its crest, under some spreading beeches, we resolved to pitch our camp, water being near at hand, and the position otherwise favourable. In a short time, the pack-horses were relieved of their loads, and neighing joyfully, they galloped away to graze in the plain we had just crossed. Our tents were pitched, and having made up our beds in them, so as to have everything ready by night-time, we began to set about preparing dinner. Wood being abundant, a roaring fire was soon blazing away cheerily, some meat we had brought from Sandy Point was put into the iron pot, together with some rice, onions, etc., and then we lay down round the fire, not a little fatigued by our day's exertions; but inhaling the grateful odours arising from the pot, with the expectant avidity of appetites which the keen Patagonian air had stimulated to an unusual extent.

By the time dinner was overnight had set in. The moon had risen, and the clear star-lit sky gave assuring promises of a continuance of fine weather. A slight breeze stirred the branches overhead, and in the distance, we could hear the lowing of the cattle on the plains, and the faint tinkling of the bells of the brood-mares. The strange novelty of the scene seemed to influence us all, and the men smoked their pipes in silence. Before going to bed I went for a short stroll to the shores of a broad lagoon which lay at the foot of the hill on which our camp was pitched. Its waters glittered brightly in the moonlight, but the woods which surrounded it were sombre and dark. Occasionally the sad plaintive cry of a grebe broke the silence, startling me not a little the first time I heard it, for it sounds exactly like the wail of a human being in pain. Going back to the camp I found my companions preparing to go to bed, an example I was not slow to follow, and soon, wrapt up in our guanaco-fur robes, with our saddles for pillows, we were all fast asleep.

It had been agreed that the next morning one of our party should go back to Sandy Point, to see how the guides were getting on, and Mr. B. having volunteered to perform that task, I rose at an early hour to get him his breakfast and see him off on his journey. Then, whilst my brother and husband went out with their guns to shoot wild-duck, I busied myself writing a few last letters to friends at home. This done, I rode down to the Straits, and had a plunge into the water, but it was so cold that I got quite numbed, and with difficulty managed to dry and dress myself. Late in the afternoon the sportsmen returned, bringing an excellent bag with them, and we speedily set about plucking a few birds, and making other preparations for dinner. Just as, that meal being over, we had settled ourselves comfortably round the fire, prepared lazily to enjoy the lovely evening, our camp-servant, who had been on the look-out for the return of Mr. B., reported that a troop of about ten horsemen were coming our way. As Indian traders do not go out to the pampas in such large parties, he was quite at a loss to imagine who the people could be who were riding out so late at night, especially as they had no pack-horses with them. We all got up and went to have a look at these mysterious horsemen. As they approached the foot of our hill, we could see that they were all armed with guns and rifles, a circumstance which began to suggest unpleasant recollections of the last Sandy Point mutiny. Could it be that another outbreak had occurred, and that these men were escaping to the pampas? If so, they might possibly make a descent on us in passing, and supply any deficiencies in their own outfit from ours. This was a rather startling state of affairs, and we were hurriedly holding counsel as to what was the best course to take under the circumstances, when our dogs suddenly started up, and began barking furiously. Then came the sound of horses' hoofs, and brushing through the tall furze, two horsemen galloped straight towards our camp, followed, as the sound of voices told us, by the rest of the party. In another second the two foremost ones reined up in front of us, turning out to be, not bloodthirsty mutineers, but Mr. Dunsmuir and Mr. Beerbohm. A few words explained all. The party was composed of some officers of the "Prinz Adalbert," a German man-of-war, which had anchored at Sandy Point that morning, Mr. B. having gone on board and invited them out to our camp for a day's shooting. Delighted at this solution of the situation, we hurried to welcome our new guests, who now arrived tired and hungry after their long ride. Among their number were H.I.H. Prince Henry of Prussia, who was on a cruise in the "Prinz Adalbert," and her commander, Captain Maclean.

Fresh logs were added to the blazing fire, meat was set to roast, soup put on to cook, and every preparation made for a good supper—an easy task, as the officers had brought plentiful supplies of all kinds of provisions with them. We then lay round the fire, the newcomers evidently quite charmed by our cosy sylvan quarters, and by the novelty of the strange picnic, which they had little anticipated making in Patagonia, of all places in the world.

I was much amused at Mr. B.'s account of how the expedition had been initiated. He had got into Sandy Point at about nine o'clock, and at ten the "Prinz Adalbert" was signalled in the offing.

As soon as she had cast anchor he went on board, having been previously acquainted with the captain, and at breakfast explained his presence in such an out-of-the-way part of the world as Sandy

Point, by an account of our intended trip, and finally asked the captain and the officers to come out to our camp and try for themselves what open-air life in Patagonia was like. He had little difficulty in persuading them to accept his offer, and whilst the officers made their preparations, he went on shore to hunt up ten horses, the number required. This was an easy matter; but it was another thing to find as many saddles, for, though many people in Sandy Point own numbers of horses, few have more than one saddle, and such being the case, they are loth to lend what at any moment may be of pressing necessity for themselves. However, by dint of ingenious combinations, some kind of an apology for a saddle was fitted to each horse, and the whole party at last set off on their trip in high spirits, and very well pleased with everything. Each officer carried a blanket or rug with him, and, as some shooting was expected, a gun and some ammunition. For the first two hours all went well, the air was warm and sunny, the scenery novel and interesting, and a zest was given to the expedition by its unconventional character and the suddenness with which it had been improvised.

But after a time, the hard action of the horses and the roughness of some of the saddles began to have their effect, especially as many of the officers were little accustomed to riding. Occasionally Mr. B. would be asked, at first in tones of implied cheerful unconcern, "How far is it to the camp?" To this question he would reply by a wave of the hand in the direction of one of the many points which shoot out along the Straits, saying, "A little beyond that point." Then, as point after point was passed, and the answer to inquiries still continued, as before, "A little beyond that point," gradually the laughter and chat which had enlivened the outset of the trip grew more constrained, occasional lapses of complete silence intervening. Now and then one of the riders would move uneasily in the saddle and sigh—and on the faces of many (especially of those who rode stirrupless saddles) fell in time an expression of fixed resignation to suffering, which was not unheroic. Mr. B. observed all this, and his conscience began to smite him. At starting, in an amiable endeavour to put everything in a rosy light, he had slightly understated the distance to our camp, and now the terrible consequences of his rashness were already visiting him. The quasi-martyrs whom he was leading, it was but too evident, were only bearing up against suffering by the comforting consciousness that they *must* be close to the camp. He could not undeceive them; he felt himself woefully wanting in courage enough to break the truth; and yet the only alternative was to go on repeating the now to him, as to everybody else, hateful formula, "A little beyond that point." His victims could only imagine one thing—that he had lost the way, though in fact he knew the road and its length only too well. Never, as he said, had it been so palpably brought before him that the way to hell is paved with good intentions; and his intentions, when mystifying the party as to the length of the road, had been of the best.

However, all things come to an end, and at last, with a feeling of deep relief, he was able to point out our hill to the weary saddle-worn band, whose advent, as possible mutineers, had thrown us into such a panic.

By the time Mr. B. had finished his story supper was ready, and that important fact having been duly announced, our hungry guests fell to, and made a hearty meal. The strain which their number put on the capabilities of our *batterie de cuisine* was fortunately relieved by a profusion of tinned provisions of all kinds which they had wisely brought with them, and under those Patagonian beeches, together with the native mutton, were discussed *asperges en jus*, which had attained their delicate flavour under the mild fostering of a Dutch summer, *patés* elaborated far away among the blue Alsatian mountains, and substantial, though withal subtly flavoured, sausages from the fatherland itself. After supper pipes were lit, and the wine-cup went round freely, the woods resounding with laughter and song till nearly midnight, by which time most of the party were beginning to feel the effects of their day's exertions, and to long for bed. In one of our tents we managed to make up four couches, on which the Prince, the Captain, Count Seckendorff, and another officer respectively laid their weary limbs, and went to sleep as best they might. The Captain, a strong stout man, had suffered more than any one from the ride, and it must have been a moot question in his secret heart whether the day's enjoyment had not been somewhat dearly purchased.

The others kept up the ball still later, and it must have been quite two o'clock before the last *convive* rolled himself up in his blanket by the fire, and silence fell over our camp. At about that hour I peered out of my tent at the scene. Round a huge heap of smouldering logs, in various attitudes, suggestive of deep repose, lay the forms of the sleepers whom chance had thus strangely thrown together for one night. Our dogs had risen from their sleep, and in their turn were making merry over whatever bones or other fragments of the feast they managed to ferret out. A few moonbeams struggled through the canopy of leaves and branches overhead, throwing strange lights and shadows over the camp, and the weird effect of the whole scene was heightened by the mysterious wail of the grebe, which at intervals came floating up in the air from the lake below, like the voice of an unquiet spirit.

CHAPTER V
Unpleasant Effects of the Wind

The sun had hardly risen the next morning ere our little camp was again astir. Making a hasty toilet I stepped out and found that our guests had all risen, and were busy in getting their guns and shooting accoutrements ready for the coming sport. As soon as they had partaken of some coffee, the whole party started off to the plains below, and for an hour or so, till their return, the repeated reports of their guns seemed to indicate that they were having good sport. Towards breakfast-time they came back, fairly satisfied with their morning's work, though I am inclined to attribute this satisfaction to their evident desire to look at everything connected with their picnic from an optimist point of view, as their bag was in reality a very small one, consisting only of a few brace of snipe and wild-duck. We then set to work to get a good breakfast ready, at which employment Prince Henry lent an intelligent hand, turning out some poached eggs in excellent style. We had a very pleasant meal, the officers expressing great regret that they were unable to prolong their stay in our beechwood quarters, the steamer being obliged to continue her journey that evening. Whilst they smoked a last pipe, the horses were driven up and saddled, and at about eight o'clock, Mr. B. and myself accompanying them as guides, they mounted and set out on the road homeward.

The stiffness consequent on their exertions of the previous day must have made the sensations they experienced on returning to the saddle anything but pleasant ones, and at the start a decidedly uncheerful spirit seemed to prevail among them; but as we cantered along, and they warmed to their work, this uneasiness disappeared, and soon all were as merry as possible. The day was lovely, and the scenery looked to the best advantage, the only drawback to our enjoyment of the ride being that the sun was rather too hot.

After we had gone several miles, we got off our horses to rest under the shade of some trees, by the side of a little stream which came bubbling out of the cool depths of the forest, emptying itself into the adjacent Straits. Here an incident occurred which might have been attended with inconvenient consequences. One of the officer's horses suddenly took it into its head to trot off, and, before anyone could stop it, disappeared round a point in the direction of Sandy Point. Mr. B. got on his horse and started in pursuit, and in the meanwhile a time of some suspense ensued, for, in the event of his being unsuccessful, some unfortunate would have had to make the best of his way on foot. However, this unpleasant contingency was happily avoided; Mr. B. soon reappeared, having managed to catch the runaway, not indeed without a great deal of trouble.

We reached Sandy Point late in the afternoon, and very glad the whole party must have been to get there, for they were most of them completely done up, and, considering the length of the ride, their rough horses and rougher saddles, this was no wonder.

After having said good-bye to the officers, with many expressions of thanks on their part for the unexpected diversion our presence in that outlandish part of the world had afforded them, Mr. B. and I immediately set out to return to the camp, which we managed to reach just as it was getting dark.

Everything was now ready for our journey, and it was resolved that we should make a start the next morning. We were therefore up early, in order to help the guides as much as possible with the packing, which was quite a formidable undertaking. It took fully three hours to get our miscellaneous goods and chattels stowed away on the pack-horses, whose number was thirteen. At last, however, all was ready; we got into the saddle, and with a last glance at the beechwood camp, which had grown quite familiar and home-like to us, we rode off, now fairly started on our journey into the unknown land that lay before us. We soon had our hands full to help the guides to keep the horses together, a rather difficult task. The mules in particular gave great trouble, and were continually leading the horses into mischief. At one time, as if by preconcerted signal, the whole troop dispersed in different directions into the wood, and there, brushing through the thick underwood, many of the pack-horses upset their packs, and trampled on the contents, whilst some of the others turned tail, and coolly trotted back to the pasture-ground they had just left at Cabo Negro.

All this was very provoking, but, with a little patience and a good deal of swearing on the part of the guides, the refractory pack-horses were re-saddled, the troop was got together again, and by dint of careful driving we at last got safely out of the wooded country, and emerged on the rolling pampa, where there was for some distance a beaten Indian track, along which the horses travelled with greater ease, till, gradually understanding what was required of them, they jogged on in front of us with tolerable steadiness and sobriety, which was only occasionally disturbed by such slight ebullitions as a free fight between two of the stallions, or an abortive attempt on the part of some hungry animal to make a dash for some particularly inviting-looking knoll of green grass at a distance off the line of our march.

The country we were now crossing was of a totally different character to that we had left behind us. Not a tree or a shrub was to be seen anywhere, and while to the left of us lay the rugged range of the Cordilleras, in front and to the right an immense plain stretched away to the horizon, rising and falling occasionally in slight undulations, but otherwise completely and monotonously level. The ground, which was rather swampy, was covered with an abundance of coarse

Collecting the "tropilla"—saddling up

green grass, amongst which we could see flocks of wild geese grazing in great numbers. We passed several freshwater lakes, covered with wild fowl, who flew up very wild at our approach. A hawk or two would occasionally hover over our heads, and once the dogs started off in pursuit of a little grey fox that had incautiously shown itself; but except these, there was no sign of animal life on the silent, seemingly interminable plain before us.

After we had ridden for several hours, we turned off to the left, facing the Cordilleras again, and soon the plain came to a sudden end, a broken country now appearing, over which we rode till nightfall, when we came in sight of the "Despuntadero," the extremity of Peckett's Harbour, an arm of the sea which runs for some distance inland. Here we were to camp for the night, and as we were all rather tired and hungry after our long ride, we urged on our horses to cover the distance that still lay between us and our camping-place as quickly as possible. But to "hasten slowly" would have been a wiser course in this case, as in most others. The rapid trot at which we now advanced disturbed the equilibrium of one of the packs, the cords holding which had already become slack, and down came the whole pack, iron pot, tin plates, and all, with an awful clatter, whilst the mare who carried it, terrified out of her wits, dashed off at a gallop, spurring with her heels her late encumbrances, and followed by the whole troop of her equally frightened companions.

The pampa was strewn with broken bags; and rice, biscuits, and other precious stores lay scattered in all directions. When we had picked up what we could, and replaced the pack on the mare, who in the meantime had been caught again, we were further agreeably surprised by the sight of another packless animal galloping over the brow of a distant hill, followed at some distance by Gregorio, who was trying to lasso it, whilst I'Aria was descried in another direction, endeavouring to collect together another scattered section of our troop. Off we scampered to aid him, turning on the way to drive up one of the mares, whom we accidentally found grazing with her foal in a secluded valley, "the guides forgetting, by the guides forgot."

By the time we got up to I'Aria, the obstinacy and speed of the refractory animals had evidently proved too much for him, since we found him sitting under a bush philosophically smoking a pipe. In answer to our query as to what had become of the horses, he waved his hand vaguely in the direction of a distant line of hills, and we were just setting off on what we feared would prove a rather arduous quest when a welcome tinkle suddenly struck our ears, and the troop reappeared from the depths of a ravine, driven up by Francisco, who had providentially come across them in time to intercept their further flight.

It was quite dark as we rode down and pitched our camp by the shore of the inlet above mentioned, under the lee of a tall bluff, not far from a little pool of fresh water. After the tents had been set up some of the men went to look for firewood, but there was a scarcity of that necessary in the region we were now in, and the little they could collect was half green. However, we managed to make a very fair fire with it, and our dinner was soon cooked and eaten, whereupon we retired to rest.

The next morning was fine, and we resolved to stop a day at our present encampment and have some shooting,—game, as Gregorio informed us, being plentiful in that region. After a light breakfast we took our guns and started off in the direction of a group of freshwater lakes which lay beyond a range of hills behind our camp. We were rewarded for our arduous climb by some excellent sport, wild geese, duck, etc., being very plentiful, and on our way back we crossed some marshy ground where there were some snipe, several brace of which we bagged. In the afternoon, it being rather hot and sultry, we refreshed ourselves with a bath in the sea, and then came dinner-time, and by half-past seven we were in bed and asleep.

The following day we continued our journey northward. A long day's ride brought us to some springs, called "Pozos de la Reina," where we camped for the night. After we had rested for a short time round the fire, and had leisure to look at one another, we became aware of a most disagreeable metamorphosis that had taken place in our faces. They were swollen to an almost unrecognisable extent, and had assumed a deep purple hue, the phenomenon being accompanied by a sharp itching. The boisterous wind which we had encountered during the day, and which is the standing drawback to the otherwise agreeable climate of Patagonia, was no doubt the cause of this annoyance, combined possibly with our salt-water bath of the day previous.

After a few days the skin of our faces peeled off completely, but the swelling did not go down for some time. I would advise any person who may make the same journey to provide themselves with masks; by taking this precaution they will save themselves a great deal of the discomfort we suffered from the winds.

The following day we left "Pozos de la Reina," and pushed forward as quickly as possible, as we had no meat left, and had not yet arrived in the country of the guanacos and ostriches. The Indians had very recently passed over all the ground we were now crossing, and, as usual, had swept away any game there might have been there.

The range where guanaco really become plentiful is about eighty miles away from Sandy Point. Still, we kept a good look-out, and any ostrich or guanaco that might have had the misfortune to show itself would have stood a poor chance of escape with some eight or nine hungry dogs and a number of not less keen horsemen at its heels.

But the day wore on, and we arrived at our destination empty-handed. The spot we camped at lay directly in front of Cape Gregorio, which was hazily visible in the distance. There was an abundance of wood in the locality, and the Indian camp being not far off, we were conveniently situated in every respect, as we intended paying these interesting people a visit before continuing our journey.

CHAPTER VI
Visit to the Indian Camp

Since we left Sandy Point our dogs had had no regular meal, and had subsisted chiefly on rice and biscuits, a kind of food which, being accustomed to meat only, was most uncongenial to their tastes and unprofitable to their bodies. For their sakes, therefore, as well as for our own, we looked forward to our visit to the Indian camp, apart from other motives of interest, in the hopes of obtaining a sufficient supply of meat to last for all of us, until we should arrive in the promised land of game.

After breakfast the horses were saddled, and taking some sugar, tobacco, and other articles for bartering purposes, we set out for the Indian camp, accompanied by Gregorio and Guillaume. I'Aria and Storer were left in charge of our camp, and Francisco went off with the dogs towards Cape Gregorio, in the hope of falling in with some stray ostrich or guanaco. The weather was fine, and for once we were able to rejoice in the absence of the rough winds which were our daily annoyance. We had not gone far when we saw a rider coming slowly towards us, and in a few minutes, we found ourselves in the presence of a real Patagonian Indian. We reined in our horses when he got close to us, to have a good look at him, and he doing the same, for a few minutes we stared at him to our hearts' content, receiving in return as minute and careful a scrutiny from him. Whatever he may have thought of us, we thought him a singularly unprepossessing object, and, for the sake of his race, we hoped an unfavourable specimen of it. His dirty brown face, of which the principal feature was a pair of sharp black eyes, was half-hidden by tangled masses of unkempt hair, held together by a handkerchief tied over his forehead, and his burly body was enveloped in a greasy guanaco-capa, considerably the worse for wear. His feet were bare, but one of his heels was armed with a little wooden spur, of curious and ingenious handiwork. Having completed his survey of our persons, and exchanged a few guttural grunts with Gregorio, of which the purport was that he had lost some horses and was on their search, he galloped away, and, glad to find some virtue in him, we were able to admire the easy grace with which he sat his well-bred looking little horse, which, though considerably below his weight, was doubtless able to do its master good service.

Continuing our way, we presently observed several mounted Indians, sitting motionless on their horses, like sentries, on the summit of a tall ridge ahead of us, evidently watching our movements. At our approach they disappeared over the ridge, on the other side of which lay their camping-ground. Cantering forward we soon came in sight of the entire Indian camp, which was pitched in a broad valley-plain, flanked on either side by steep bluffs, and with a little stream flowing down its centre. There were about a dozen big hide tents, in front of which stood crowds of men and women, watching our approach with lazy curiosity. Numbers of little children were disporting themselves in the stream, which we had to ford in order to get to the tents. Two Indians, more inquisitive than their brethren, came out to meet us, both mounted on the same horse, and saluted us with much grinning and jabbering. On our arrival in the camp, we were soon encircled by a curious crowd, some of whose number gazed at us with stolid gravity, whilst others laughed and gesticulated as they discussed our appearance in their harsh guttural language, with a vivacious manner which was quite at variance with the received traditions of the solemn bent of the Indian mind. Our accoutrements and clothes seemed to excite great interest, my riding-boots in particular being objects of attentive examination, and apparently of much serious speculation. At first they were content to observe them from a distance, but presently a little boy was delegated by the elders, to advance and give them a closer inspection. This he proceeded to do, coming towards me with great caution, and when near enough, he stretched out his hand and touched the boots gently with the tips of his fingers. This exploit was greeted with roars of laughter and ejaculations, and emboldened by its success, many now ventured to follow his example, some enterprising spirits extending their researches to the texture of my ulster, and one even going so far as to take my hand in his, whilst subjecting a little bracelet I wore to a profound and exhaustive scrutiny.

Indian camp.

Whilst they were thus occupied, I had leisure to observe their general appearance. I was not struck so much by their height as by their extraordinary development of chest and muscle. As regards their stature, I do not think the average height of the men exceeded six feet, and as my husband stands six feet two inches, I had a favourable opportunity for forming an accurate estimate. One or two there were, certainly, who towered far above him, but these were exceptions. The women were mostly of the ordinary height, though I noticed one who must have been quite six feet, if not more. The features of the pure-bred Tehuelche are extremely regular, and by no means unpleasant to look at. The nose is generally aquiline, the mouth well shaped and beautified by the whitest of teeth, the expression of the eye is intelligent, and the form of the whole head affords a favourable index to their mental capabilities. These remarks do not apply to the Tehuelches in whose veins there is a mixture of Araucanian or Fuegian blood. The flat noses, oblique eyes, and badly proportioned figures of the latter make them most repulsive objects, and they are as different from a pure-bred Tehuelche in every respect as "Wheel-of-Fortune" from an ordinary carthorse. Their hair is long and coarse, and is worn parted in the middle, being prevented from falling over their faces by means of a handkerchief, or fillet of some kind, tied round the forehead. They have naturally little hair on the face, and such growth as may appear is carefully eradicated, a painful operation, which many extend even to their eyebrows. Their dress is simple, and consists of a "chiripá," a piece of cloth round the loins, and the indispensable guanaco capa, which is hung loosely over the shoulders and held round the body by the hand, though it would obviously seem more convenient to have it secured round the waist with a belt of some kind. Their horse-hide boots are only worn, for reasons of economy, when hunting. The women dress like the men except as regards the chiripá, instead of which they wear a loose kind of gown beneath the capa, which they fasten at the neck with a silver brooch or pin. The children are allowed to run about naked till they are five or six years old and are then dressed like their elders. Partly for ornament, partly also as a means of protection against the wind, a great many Indians paint their faces, their favourite colour, as far as I could see, being red, though one or two I observed had given the preference to a mixture of that colour with black, a very diabolical appearance being the result of this combination.

The Tehuelches are a race that is fast approaching extinction, and even at present it scarcely numbers eight hundred souls. They lead a rambling nomadic existence, shifting their camping places from one region to another, whenever the game in their vicinity gets shy or scarce. It is fortunate for them that the immense numbers of guanaco and ostriches makes it an easy matter for them to find subsistence, as they are extremely lazy, and, plentiful as game is around them, often pass two or three days without food rather than incur the very slight exertion attendant on a day's hunting.

But it is only the men who are cursed or blessed with this indolent spirit. The women are indefatigably industrious. All the work of Tehuelche existence is done by them except hunting. When not employed in ordinary household work, they busy themselves in making guanaco capas, weaving gay-coloured garters and fillets for the hair, working silver ornaments, and so forth. Not one of their least arduous tasks is that of collecting firewood, which, always a scarce article, becomes doubly hard to find, except by going great distances, when they camp long in one place.

But though treated thus unfairly as regards the division of labour, the women can by no means complain of want of devotion to them on the part of the men. Marriages are matters of great solemnity with them, and the tie is strictly kept. Husband and wife show great affection for one another, and both agree in extravagant love of their offspring, which they pet and spoil to their hearts' content.

The most prominent characteristic of the Tehuelche is his easy-going good humour, for whereas most aboriginal races incline to silence and saturnine gravity, he is all smiles and chatter. The other good qualities of the race are fast disappearing under the influence of "aguardiente[1]" to the use of which they are getting more and more addicted, and soon, it is to be feared, they will become nothing more than a pack of impoverished, dirty, thieving ragamuffins.

After having sat for some time on horseback, in the centre of the numerous circle above referred to, we dismounted, the act causing fresh animation and merriment in our interviewers, whose interest in us, after a thorough examination, had begun to flag somewhat. An object which greatly excited their feelings was a rifle belonging to my brother, and their delight knew no bounds when he dismounted and fired it off for their edification once or twice at a distant mark. At each discharge they set up a lusty howl of satisfaction, and nothing would do for them but for each to be allowed to handle the weapon and inspect its mechanism. There was a trader in the camp who had arrived about the same time as we did, and amongst other wares he had brought a rusty carbine with him for sale. He was called upon by the Indians to produce it and fire it off to compare its qualities with those of my brother's rifle. This he proceeded to do, but seven times in succession the cartridges missed fire. Each time this happened he was greeted with shouts of derisive laughter, and it was evident that both he and his weapon were the objects of most disparaging remarks on the part of the Tehuelches. One of them, a man of some humour, brought out a small piece of ostrich meat and offered it to the trader in exchange for his carbine, saying in broken Spanish, "Your gun never kill piece of meat as big as this. Your gun good to kill dead guanaco." At which witticism there was renewed and prolonged applause, as the newspapers say.

But excitement reached its height when I produced the bag of sugar we had brought, and began to distribute small handfuls of its contents among the children. Everybody pressed round me—men and women, hustling and pushing in their eagerness to get some of

1. Alcoholic drink

the coveted dainty. I was obliged to be careful in my bounty, however, or we should not have enough left to obtain any meat in exchange, and a great many sweet-toothed Tehuelches had to remain disappointed in consequence. As it was, we found considerable difficulty in obtaining any meat. The Indians had not been out hunting for three days, and there was hardly anything but pemmican in the camp,—a greasy concoction, with which we by no means cared to experiment on our stomachs. With difficulty we at last succeeded in obtaining the leg and breast of an ostrich, and a small piece of half sun-dried guanaco meat, which looked extremely untempting. This transaction having been accomplished, we wandered leisurely about the camp, glancing at the different objects of interest that came in our way, pestered not a little as we moved along by swarms of yelping curs, which barked and snapped viciously at us, and could only be kept at a respectful distance by a free use of stones and whips. At one of the tents, we saw two remarkably clean and pretty girls, who were engaged on some kind of sewing work; and beside them—probably making love to one (or both)—stood an equally good-looking youth, who struck me by the peculiar neatness of his dress, and his general "*tiré à quatre epingles*" appearance. His hair was brushed and combed, and carefully parted,—a bright red silk handkerchief keeping its glossy locks in due subjection. His handsome guanaco capa was new, and brilliantly painted on the outside, and being half opened, displayed a clean white chiripá, fastened at the waist by a silver belt of curious workmanship. A pair of neatly fitting horse-hide boots encased his feet, reaching up to the knees, where they were secured by a pair of gay-coloured garters, possibly the gift of one of the fair maidens at his side.

Struck by his graceful bearing and well-bred looking face, I begged Mr. B., who had brought a sketch-book with him, to make a sketch of this handsome son of the pampa. During the process the young Indian never moved, and preserved a perfectly indifferent demeanour; but when the picture was finished, and given to him for inspection, his forehead contracted with anger, an expression of fear came in his eyes; he gave vent to some angry sounding gutturals, and finally, much to our annoyance, tore the portrait to pieces. He was under the impression that the object of making the sketch was to throw some evil spell over him, and that a misfortune would happen if it were not destroyed. Being relieved of this danger, his feelings regained their natural calm, and he grinned contentedly at our evident wrath at his high-handed proceeding.

The Indians were about to make their annual visit to Sandy Point, where they go to obtain the rations of sugar, tobacco, etc., allowed to them by the Chilian Government, and to barter with the inhabitants for the luxuries of civilisation, in exchange for furs and ostrich feathers, at which transactions, as they are seldom sober during their stay outside the colony, they generally get worsted by the cunning white man. Our curiosity regarding the Indians being satisfied and having obtained all the meat we could from them, we now turned homewards.

CHAPTER VII
The Prairie Fire

As we rode along, our attention was attracted by a faint smell of burning, and presently thick clouds of smoke came rolling towards us. We pressed wonderingly on, anxious to discover the whereabouts of the fire, which we trusted lay somewhere far from our camp. Reaching a slight eminence, we were able to command a view of the country ahead. A cry of dismay escaped our lips as we looked around, and drawing rein, we stared blankly at one another. A fearful sight lay before us. To our left, right in front, and gradually wreathing the hills to our right, a huge prairie fire came rushing rapidly along. Dense masses of smoke curled aloft, and entirely obscured the sky; the flames, which shot fiercely up, cast a strange yellow glare over everything. Even whilst we watched, a strong gust of wind swept the fire with incredible swiftness towards us, and in a second we were enveloped in such a dense cloud of smoke that we were unable to see one another. The situation had now become critical, and not a moment was to be lost. Half choked and bewildered by the suddenness with which the danger had come upon us, we scarcely knew what course to take. Already our horses were snorting with fear, as the crackling of the burning grass and bushes came nearer and nearer. To run away from the coming fire was useless; the alternative was to face it at a gallop and get through it if possible. To throw our guanaco mantles over our heads and draw them as tightly round us as we could, was the work of a second, and then digging our spurs into our horses, we dashed forward, every one for himself. The moments that followed seemed an eternity. As I urged my unwilling horse forward, the sense of suffocation grew terrible, I could scarcely draw breath, and the panting animal seemed to stagger beneath me. The horrible crackling came nearer and nearer; I became conscious of the most intolerable heat, and my head began to swim round. My horse gave two or three furious plunges, and then burst madly forward. Almost choked, come what might, I could bear the mantle over my head no longer, and tore it off me. The sudden sense of relief that came over me as I did so, I shall never forget. I looked up, the air was comparatively clear, and the fire *behind* me. By some miracle I had passed through it unhurt! I looked for my companions, and, to my inexpressible joy, saw them emerge one by one from the black mass of smoke, which was now rapidly receding into the distance. Congratulations and exclamations over, we retraced our steps to try and discover how we had managed to escape so luckily. The reason was soon apparent. By a piece of fortune, we had happened to ride over a narrow pebbly tract of ground, where the grass was extremely sparse, and where there were but few bushes; had chance led us over any other track, where the grass was thick and tall, we could scarcely ever have got through the danger. Our poor horses had suffered a good deal as it was, their feet and legs being scorched and singed severely.

Our thoughts now flew to our camp, and to Storer and I'Aria, whom we had left behind there. That they had escaped we had little doubt, but for our tents and chattels we felt there was no hope. The landscape seemed completely changed by the fire, all around, as far as we could see, stretched black smoking plains, and the outlines of the hills had become quite unfamiliar to us.

With rather heavy hearts we pushed forward, eagerly scanning the country for some indication which might guide us to the quarter where our camp had stood. If, as we had every reason to believe, our things were burnt, our Patagonian trip was at an end, for the present, at all events. Fortunately, things did not turn out so badly. Presently my husband, who was riding in advance of the others, gave a shout, and made signals for us to come on. I need hardly say that we did not lose a moment in joining him, and a welcome sight, as we got up to him, met our eyes. Some two or three hundred yards below the hill on which we were, we perceived our little white tents standing safe and unharmed on a narrow green tract of land, which looked like a smiling island in the midst of the vast black plain. Storer and I'Aria, too, we could see moving about, and overjoyed, we galloped down towards them, they running out to meet us, having suffered no little anxiety, on their parts, as to what might have happened to us. We pressed question after question to I'Aria and Storer as to how they had managed to save the camp. Storer was unable to give any intelligible account, so entirely upset was he by fright, but I'Aria's natural philosophical calm had not deserted him, even on this occasion, and from him we heard all particulars. The fire, he informed us, had been caused by the Indian we had met in the morning on the look-out for strayed horses. This man had amused himself by setting fire to the long dry grass in various places, and, fanned by a strong wind, the flames spread, and soon assumed enormous proportions.

Quick to perceive the possible danger our camp was in, the Indian at once galloped up, and with the assistance of I'Aria and Storer, set about making a "contra-fuego" or counter fire, that is to say, they gradually set fire to the grass all-round the camp, letting it burn a considerable tract, but always keeping it well in subjection, beating it out with bushes and trampling it under foot, so that it could not get beyond their control. This precautionary measure was fortunately completed by the time the big fire came on, and although, for a minute or two, they were half suffocated by the smoke, the fire passed harmlessly by the camp itself, the burnt belt around it proving an effectual safeguard.

Our horses were all safe, as they had been grazing on the far side of a stream in an adjacent valley. The camp was in great disorder; the tents were blackened by the smoke, the provision-bags and other chattels lay scattered in confusion. Our furs and rugs had been used to cover the cartridges with, for, whilst the fire raged around it, the camp was deluged with showers of sparks, and an explosion might easily have occurred, had this precaution not been taken. For some time, we were busy putting things straight, and in the meanwhile François arrived from his hunting excursion. It had proved unsuccessful; and as we had obtained but very little meat from the Indians, for the sake of our dogs, who had been on very short rations for some time, it became a matter of great urgency that we should get as soon as possible into regions where guanaco and ostrich were plentiful, and accordingly we decided to start on the following day. Dinner over, my companions were not long before they went to sleep, but feeling little inclination to follow their example, I strolled out, and wandered round the camp, watching with interest the strange changes that came over the landscape as day waned and night came slowly on. The black hills behind the camp loomed like shadowy phantoms against the sky; far and wide slept the silent pampa, its undulating surface illumined by the rays of a lovely moon. The faint glow which tinged the horizon, and the strange noises which a puff of wind occasionally brought to my ears, showed that the mighty fire was still burning in the distance with unbated fury, perhaps not to stop in its devastating course till it reached the sea-coast.

For a long time I stood immersed in the contemplation of this weird desolate scene, giving myself up to the mysterious feelings and the many vague and fanciful thoughts it suggested, till, overcome with the excitement and exertions of the day, I had at last to give way to drowsiness and seek my couch.

CHAPTER VIII
Unpleasant Visitors

The next morning, we were up betimes, as we were going to continue our journey. Whilst we were engaged in the tedious operation of packing up, an Indian woman walked suddenly into the ring of bushes which surrounded our encampment and seated herself silently by the fire. Gregorio elicited from her that on the previous night the Indians had been drinking heavily, and that she had had a quarrel with her husband whilst both were inebriated, in consequence of which she had left his tent, and was now on her way to Sandy Point. She had walked the whole distance from the Indian camp barefoot but did not seem in the least tired. I suppose she counted on her husband's regretting his behaviour, and coming after her to fetch her back, for she could hardly have seriously entertained the idea of walking all the way to Sandy Point. I offered her some biscuits and a stick of chocolate, which she accepted readily enough, but without even so much as a grunt by way of thanks. Presently she told Gregorio that the Indians were breaking up their camp, and that some were going to march on to Sandy Point. This piece of information made us hurry on with our work, as we dreaded being surprised by a party of Indians, with all our effects scattered about, offering tempting facilities for abstraction, which the Tehuelche heart was sure not to be able to resist. To such a visit we were moreover extremely liable, as our camp was unfortunately close to the trail to Sandy Point.

Our fears were realised only too soon, for about a quarter of an hour after the arrival of the squaw two Indians came crashing unceremoniously through the bushes; and wheeling their horses about the camp, careless of our crockery, after a short examination they dismounted, and coolly sat down by our fire, answering our angry looks with unperturbed stares of stolid indifference. Five minutes later another party arrived, followed shortly by a further batch, and presently we were quite inundated by a swarm of these unbidden guests. Of course, our work was stopped, all our attention being required to look after our goods and chattels. Over these we kept guard in no very good humour, breathing fervent prayers the while for speedy relief from our friends, who on their part evinced no particular hurry to go away. They had made themselves comfortable at our fire and were passing round the social pipe in evident good humour with themselves and their present quarters. To complete the irony of the situation, one of their number who could speak Spanish came and asked me for a little coffee, which he purposed to cook in our kettle, which was still simmering conveniently on the fire. As may be imagined, he met with an indignant refusal; however, it only appeared to amuse him and his friends, and by no means influenced them in hastening their departure.

Meanwhile time went on, and some expedient for getting rid of them had to be devised unless we wished to lose a whole day. It occurred to us that they might possibly be bribed to go away by means of a small offering of whisky; and through Gregorio we accordingly intimated to them that if they would leave us they should be rewarded for their kindness with a glass of that spirit. To our relief they accepted this offer, and we presently had the satisfaction of seeing them ride leisurely away. To do them justice, I must say that contrary to our fears, they did not steal any of our effects, though possibly the strict watch we kept over them may have had something to do with this unusual display of honesty.

The moment they had gone we redoubled our efforts and succeeded in getting all our horses saddled and packed without further molestation. The three mules still remained to be packed, but these we left to the care of Gregorio and Guillaume who were to follow us, we, meanwhile, starting off under the guidance of old I'Aria. Francisco went off alone, by another route, in order to forage for meat, be it ostrich or guanaco, of which both ourselves and the dogs stood very much in need, the small supply we had got from the Indians being quite exhausted.

Just as we were leaving an Indian galloped up, who turned out to be the husband of the pedestrian squaw, who, after the departure of the other Indians, still remained in our camp. The reconciliation scene was a very short one and did not go beyond a few inexpressive grunts on either side, after which the squaw got up on horseback behind her husband, and off they rode towards Sandy Point.

We now struck northwards, leaving Cape Gregorio, which lay directly opposite our late encampment, at our backs. I'Aria having to keep the troop together singlehanded we had plenty to do to help him, and in galloping after refractory horses, urging on the lazy ones, and occasionally stopping to adjust packs, the time passed quickly enough. We occasionally crossed tracts of land covered with a plant bearing a profusion of red berries of the cranberry species. They were quite ripe now, and we found them pleasant and refreshing. The weather was, as usual, sunny and bracing; and except that as yet we had not seen a guanaco or given chase to a single ostrich, we had nothing to grumble about. I'Aria told us that we were certain to meet with guanaco on that day's march, so, with this assurance, we comforted ourselves and kept a sharp look-out, eagerly scanning the horizon of each successive plain, and woe betide the unfortunate animal that might appear within our ken. The day passed, however, and a dark patch of beeches, which stood near the spot where we were to camp that night, appeared in view without our having seen either an ostrich or a guanaco. Somebody found an ostrich egg though, and it was carefully kept against dinner-time, for although it must have been laid two or perhaps three months, there was still a possibility of its being tolerably good, as these eggs occasionally keep till the month of April, six months after laying time.

Towards sunset we arrived at a broad valley scattered over with picturesque clumps of beeches and bordered on its far side by a thick wood of the same tree. I'Aria pointed out a spot to us where he said there were some springs, by the side of which we were to camp, and thither we accordingly rode. But when we got there no springs were to be seen, and I'Aria said he must have mistaken the place. He suddenly remembered, however, that a conspicuous clump of beeches, some way up the valley, marked the right spot, so we turned in that direction. But again, was I'Aria mistaken, and when—following various of his sudden inspirations—we had wandered about the valley in all directions for a considerable time without coming across these problematic springs, we began to think ourselves justified in presuming that I'Aria had lost his way, and in charging him with the same. He denied the accusation, however, with a calm and steady assurance, which, considering that all the time he was leading us about in aimless helplessness, would have had something rather humorous about it had our situation been a less serious one. If we did not succeed in finding the springs, besides having to endure the torture of thirst ourselves we should have to stop up all night to look after the horses, who would be certain to go off in search of water and get lost. It was rapidly getting dark too, and there were no signs of the arrival of any of the other guides, whose absence was a further confirmation that we could not be on the right track. As a last resource we resolved to separate, and each go in a different direction in search of water, though I must say we had little hopes of success, it being known to us that beyond the springs in question there was no other water in that part of the country for a considerable distance. Hurling bitter but useless anathemas at I'Aria, who was now confidently pointing out a new spot as the "really" right one, we accordingly broke up, and having arranged to fire a shot as a signal, should any one of us find water, dispersed over the valley in all directions.

I had hardly skirted the beechwood for more than a minute or so when my horse suddenly neighed joyfully, and in an opening among the trees I saw two or three small pools of spring water. Overjoyed, I lost no time in firing off my gun, the report of which soon brought up all the others, who had not gone far. In justice to I'Aria it must be said that for the last hour he had been wandering about close to where the springs lay, and his persistent denial of having lost his way was so far justified. Besides, as there was no trail of any description across the pampa over which we had that day ridden, it was really no easy matter to hit on the right spot immediately.

We had just set up the tents and made the fire when Gregorio and Guillaume, at whose prolonged absence, now that we were at the springs ourselves, we had become rather uneasy, appeared with the mules. They had been delayed on the road by the packs getting undone. Francisco too soon came up, and though he had been unsuccessful in the chase, he arrived in time to cook an excellent omelette for our dinners with the ostrich egg, which turned out to be perfectly sound and palatable.

The next day was to be devoted to guanaco-hunting, the want of meat having become quite a serious matter; our dogs were getting weak, and our stores, on which we had to rely solely for food, were disappearing in an alarmingly quick manner.

It is marvellous how the ordinary excitement of hunting is increased when, as in our case, one's dinner depends on one's success; and it was with feelings almost of solemnity, that early in the morning we selected and saddled our best horses, sharpened our hunting-knives, slung our rifles, and, followed by the dogs, who knew perfectly well that real earnest sport was meant, threaded the beechwood and rode up on to the plateau, where, according to the unanimous assurance of the guides, we could not fail to meet with guanaco.

I'Aria and Storer having been left behind to look after the camp, our hunting-party numbered seven. In order to cover as much ground as possible we spread out in a line, extending over about two miles, and in this order we cantered northward from the valley, carefully scanning the plain, which stretched flat away for a good distance, but apparently as bare of guanaco as it was of grass. The weather, unlike that of the preceding day, was very cold, and a bitterly sharp wind blew right into our faces, making those of our number who had neglected to bring their greatcoats or furs very uncomfortable. This, however, was a trifling matter, if only those good guanacos would obligingly make their appearance! But evidently nothing was farther from their minds, and we rode over the plain, mile after mile, with hopes which, like the thermometer, were gradually sinking towards zero. As time went on, the haze which bound the plateau at our approach solidified itself into an escarpment. In due time this was reached, and I rode up it, expecting to find another plain on its summit as usual. Instead, however, a broken, hilly country appeared in view, crossed in all directions by ravines. I looked eagerly about, but still no guanaco. Our line of advance, meantime, lost its order, owing to the changed nature of the ground, and frequently I lost sight of all my companions, as I descended into a ravine, or rode round the base of some tall hillock; but it was never long before I caught a glimpse of one or other of them again.

The wind got colder and colder, a white cloud crept up on the horizon, and grew and grew, sweeping swiftly towards me, till I suddenly found myself enveloped in a furious hail-storm. I came to a standstill and covered up my head to protect myself from the hailstones, which were very large. The squall did not last long, but when I looked up again I found the whole country was whitened over, an atmospheric freak having created a dreary winter landscape in the middle of summer. Suddenly I started; close to me stood, perfectly motionless, and staring me full in the face, a tall guanaco. I was so startled and surprised that for the space of a minute I sat quietly returning his stare. A movement of my horse broke the spell. The guanaco darted up the side of a hill like lightning, and pausing a moment on its summit, disappeared. I meanwhile had unslung my rifle and was off in pursuit of him. Instead of climbing the hill, I rode quickly round its base, and on the other side, as I had expected, I discovered my friend looking upward, no doubt thinking I should appear by the same road he had come. I had the selfishness, though I am sure sportsmen will excuse it, to wish to kill the first guanaco myself, and I was therefore by no means displeased to find that my companions had not as yet perceived us. With a beating heart I dismounted and walked slowly towards the guanaco, who, though he saw me coming, still remained quietly standing. My weapon was a light rook-rifle, but though an excellent arm, it did not carry more than 150 yards with precision, and I was now something over 180 yards from my prey. He allowed me to advance till within the required distance, but then, to my disgust, just as I was preparing to fire, leisurely walked on another thirty or forty yards before he stopped again, watching me the while, as it seemed with an amused look of impertinence, which aggravated me considerably. I slowly followed him, vowing to fire the moment I was within range, whether he moved or not. This time I was more successful. The guanaco allowed me to come within about the necessary 150 yards. "Poor fellow!" I murmured generously, as I brought my rifle up to my shoulder and took aim just behind his. Only one step forward to make quite certain. Alas! I took it, and down I went into a hole, which in my eagerness I had not noticed, falling rather heavily on my face. In a second I was up again, just in time to see the guanaco bounding up a far escarpment, taking with him my chance of becoming the heroine of the day. There was nothing for it but to walk back to where I had left my horse and see what had become of my companions.

I took the same road the guanaco had taken on the remote possibility of falling in with him again. Riding up the escarpment above referred to, I came on to a broad plain, and there an exciting chase was going on, in which, as it appeared, I was condemned to take the part of a spectator only. At some distance, and going across my line of sight, was a guanaco running at full speed, closely followed by a pack of dogs, in whose track, but some way behind, galloped three horsemen, whom I made out to be my husband, and brother, and Gregorio. The guanaco at first seemed to be losing ground, but it was only for an instant; in another he bounded away with ease, and it was apparent that as yet he was only playing with his pursuers. The pace soon began to tell on the dogs; the less speedy were already beginning to tail off, one of them, probably Gregorio's swift Pié-de-Plata, being far in advance of its comrades, and by no means to be shaken off by the guanaco, who had now given up any playful demonstrations of superiority and had settled down to run in good earnest.

On, on they go—quarry, dogs, horsemen, will soon be out of sight. But what's this? The guanaco has stopped! Only for a moment, though. But he has swerved to the left, and behind him a new dog and horseman have appeared on the scene, emerging, as if by magic, from the bowels of the earth. The chase is now better under my view. If some lucky chance would only bring the guanaco my way! The fresh dog is evidently discomforting him, and his having had to swerve has brought all the other dogs a good bit nearer to his heels. But on he goes, running bravely, and making for the escarpment, for in the hilly country below he knows he is at an advantage The dogs seem to be aware of this too, for they redouble their efforts, a splendid race ensuing. Suddenly another horseman appears on the plateau, and the unfortunate guanaco must again swerve to the left, a movement which, hurrah! brings him almost facing towards where I am standing. That is to say, he must cross the escarpment at some point on a line between myself and the newcomer, the other horsemen, from the manner the race had been run, forming a circle in his rear, which debarred his escape in any other direction. Seeing this, wild with excitement, I dug my spurs into my horse, and flew along the edge of the escarpment, the horseman on the other side doing the same, in order to shut out the guanaco and throw him back on his foes behind. Seeing his last chance about to be cut off, he redoubled his efforts to get through between us. On, on we strain. Nearer and nearer, he gets to the edge of the plain, and already, with despair, I see that I shall be too late. But faster even than the swift guanaco, a gallant black hound has crept up, and in another instant, though the former dashes past me within a yard of my horse's nose and disappears over the side of the escarpment, the good dog has already made its spring, and, clinging like grim death to the guanaco's haunch, vanishes with him.

After them, in another instant, swept the whole quarry of dogs, and by the time I reined in, and got my horse down the steep ravine-side, they had thrown the guanaco, which Pié-de-Plata had brought to a standstill below; and Francisco, the horseman who had last appeared on the plateau, and at so opportune a moment, had already given the *coup-de-grace* with his knife.

One after another the other hunters gradually arrived, their horses more or less blown; and whilst pipes were lit and flasks produced, we had leisure to examine this, our first guanaco. Looking at his frame, his long, powerful legs, his deep chest, and body as fine-drawn almost as a greyhound's, we no longer wondered that guanacos run as swiftly as they do. Indeed, this one would have laughed at us, had he not been closed in as he was. The fur of the full-grown guanaco is of a woolly texture, and in colour of a reddish brown on the back, the neck, and the quarters; being whitish on the belly and the inner sides of the legs. The head closely resembles that of a camel; the eyes, which have a strange look on account of the peculiar shape of the eye bones, are very large and beautiful. A fair-sized guanaco weighs from 180 to 200 pounds.

Meantime, Gregorio having begun to cut up the guanaco, to our chagrin it was discovered to be mangy—a disease very common among these animals, probably on account of the brackishness of the water; and the meat being consequently unfit for food, we abandoned it to the dogs, who now made the first good meal they had had since we left Sandy Point. They were soon gorged to such an extent that they became useless for hunting purposes, and we had therefore to ride on, now relying solely on our rifles.

Gregorio had seen a herd of guanacos at the far end of the plain over which the chase had taken place, and thither we accordingly rode. After half an hour's galloping, we reached its limit, finding below a broad valley broken up into various depressions and hillocks. At the base of one of the latter we saw a small herd of guanaco, within range of which, by dint of careful stalking, we presently managed to come. Two fortunate shots brought a couple of their number down, and luckily both turned out to be quite healthy. Under the skilful manipulation of Gregorio and Francisco, in a marvellously short space of time they were cut up, and the meat having been distributed among our various saddles, heavily laden, we turned homewards.

Guanacos

The way back seemed terribly long, now that we had no longer the excitement of hunting to shorten the time; and it seemed quite incredible that we had gone the distance we had been, when, towards sunset, after a cold and weary ride, we at last stood on the edge of the plain which overlooked the valley where lay our home for the nonce.

The evening had turned out fine, the boisterous wind which had annoyed us so much in the daytime had died away, and the sky was now bright and clear. Through the branches of the beech trees I could catch a glimpse of our camp, with its white tents just peeping over the green bushes, and a thin column of blue smoke rising up into the air, pleasantly suggestive of warm tea and other comforts awaiting us. Farther on, in the long green grass of the valley, which was now glowing under the last rays of the sun, were our horses, some grazing, others lying stretched out, lazily enjoying their day's respite from work, whilst the colts and fillies, as is their wont at sundown, were frisking about and kicking up their heels in all the exuberance of youth, unconscious as yet of heavy packs and sharp spurs. Whatever special character the peaceful scene might otherwise want was fully supplied by the picturesquely wild appearance of my companions, as, eschewing contemplation, and anticipating dinner, they rode quickly ahead towards the camp on their shaggy, sturdy horses, their bodies muffled in the graceful guanaco robe, and huge pieces of red raw meat dangling on either side of their saddles, followed by the blood-stained hounds, who seemed thoroughly tired after their hard day's work.

But whatever country one is in, whatever scenes one may be among—in one's own cosy snuggery in England, or in the bleak steppes of Patagonia—there is a peculiar sameness in the feeling that comes over one towards the hours of evening, and which inevitably calls up the thought, It must be getting near dinner-time. Yielding to this admonition, which to-day was by no means less plain than usual, I quitted my eyrie and rode down to the camp.

When I got there, I found preparations for an ample meal in full swing. Ingeniously spitted on a wooden stave, the whole side of a guanaco was roasting before a blazing fire, and in the pot a head of the same animal was yielding its substance towards the production of what I was assured would turn out an excellent soup. At dinner-time I was able practically to confirm this assurance; a better broth cannot be concocted than that obtained from such a guanaco head, with the addition of rice, dried vegetables, chilis, etc. But, at the risk of incurring the charge of digressing too much on the subject of eating, I must pay a tribute to the delicacy of a peculiar morsel in the guanaco, which we called "Fat-behind-the-Eye," and which is, in fact, a piece of fat situated as indicated by its name. The tongue and the brain are rare tit-bits, but they must yield in subtle savouriness to the aforesaid *bonne-bouche*. Having once tasted it, till the end of our trip guanaco head formed a standing item in our daily messes, and whatever other culinary novelties we discussed, and they were as numerous as strange, "Fat-behind-the-eye" always retained its supremacy in our affections as the *ne plus ultra* of pampa delicacies.

CHAPTER IX
Laguna Blanca and an Earthquake

We should like to have lingered on in the beechwood valley, but the necessity of pushing forward as quickly as possible was too urgent to allow of our indulging in our lazy desires, and daybreak saw our party once more in the saddle.

The country over which we rode this day was more rugged and hilly than any we had crossed previously; the sun shone down upon us in all the intensity of its summer heat, and the glare of the hot dry ground affected our eyes painfully as we rode along.

"How far have we still to go?" was a question which was often on our lips, though, from experience, we might have known that whatever answer we got from the guides, we should be no wiser than before. They would reply glibly enough, four or five leagues, as the case might be, but we had found that their ideas of a league were most elastic, appearing to vary daily, and to an extent which made it impossible for us to form any mean average even, to guide us to an approximate estimation of the value of their assertions. Thus, a league might mean ten miles to-day, and to-morrow possibly only one.

At length, as the sun was beginning to sink, a shout from one of the guides made us glance wearily up. We found ourselves on the brow of an escarpment, at the foot of which extended a far-stretching plain, in the midst of which, shimmering like a sheet of silver, lay a broad lake, called "Laguna Blanca," or the White Lake.

This welcome sight at once revived our drooping spirits, and for the next hour we rode merrily forward, following Gregorio, who was seeking for a little ravine, where there was a small freshwater stream which flowed down towards the lake. We soon came upon it and lost no time in jumping out of the saddle and setting to work with a will, at the erection of our tents and the preparation of our evening meal. The latter having been discussed, we went to bed.

The sun was rather high in the heavens when I opened my eyes the next morning, and, pulling aside the flap of the tent, looked out upon the scene. All our camp was still wrapped in sleep save I'Aria, who was sitting over the fire smoking his pipe, whilst he watched the kettle boiling, in placid expectation of his morning coffee. The plains below were silent; but the air was noisy with the cries of the flocks of geese and wild duck, who were winging their flight from the lake towards the rich fields of cranberries farther inland. The sharp quack of the ibis would occasionally startle me, as a bevy of these birds passed seemingly just over my head, but, in reality, far up in the air.

From the contemplation of this scene, I was suddenly and rudely awakened. A loud rumbling sound rose on the air; and, before I had time to wonder what it could mean, a heaving of the ground, resembling a sea-swell, sent me flying on my back, and, as by magic, the silent camp became alive with shouts of fear and wonder, as everybody rushed out of the tents in dismay. The shocks occurred again and again, but each time weaker, and in about five minutes they had ceased altogether, but it was some time before we recovered our equanimity. This was the first time I had ever experienced an earthquake, and such a sickly sensation of helplessness as comes over one during the heaving up and down of the earth would, I should think, be hard to equal. Our guides told us that none of them had ever felt an earthquake in Patagonia before, nor had they ever heard of one having taken place.

Later on, on our return to Sandy Point, we learnt that the earthquake had caused a good deal of disaster in the colony. All the bottles and stores in Pedro's shop were thrown from their shelves and broken, and there were few inhabitants in the colony who did not sustain some similar loss.

As may be imagined, the earthquake provided us with matter for conversation for some time, and in that respect, at least, was a not unwelcome occurrence.

Breakfast over, it was agreed that we should separate into two parties, one for the purpose of ostrich-hunting, whilst the other should devote its energies to the pursuit of the guanaco. My husband and Mr. B. preferring the latter chase, rode off with their rifles, together with Gregorio and Guillaume, towards the hilly country we had crossed the day before.

As soon as they were gone my brother and I, with François, started off along a ridge of hills which exactly faced our camp, and which sloped down into the plains below. We were followed by four ostrich hounds and were mounted on the best and fleetest horses we could select out of our tropilla. The little animal that I bestrode could not have exceeded fifteen hands. He was a high-spirited little bay with a white blaze down his face, and three white legs. He would clamber up precipitous places where the stones and rocks crumbled and gave way beneath his feet, or canter down a steep decline, and jump the wide gullies with the greatest ease. As we galloped along the smoother ground which intervened between the hills, and which was deeply undermined by hundreds of holes of the "tuca-tuca" (prairie rat), his activity in avoiding a fall astonished me. My brother was equally well mounted on a long, low, clever black, who had the reputation of great speed; while François rode a well-shaped brown, with handsome arching neck and tiny head.

As we rode silently along, with our eyes well about us, in the hopes of sighting an ostrich, my horse suddenly shied at something white lying on the ground at a few paces distant. Throwing the reins over his head, I dismounted and walked towards the spot. Amongst some long grass I discovered a deserted nest of an ostrich containing ten or eleven eggs, and calling François to examine them, was greatly chagrined to find that none of them were fresh. With the superstition of an ostrich-hunter François picked up a feather lying close at hand, and sticking it in his cap, assured us that this was a good sign, and that it would not be long before we came across one of these birds.

His prediction was speedily verified, for on reaching the summit of a little hill, up which we had slowly and stealthily proceeded, two small grey objects suddenly struck my eye. I signed to François and my brother, who were riding some twenty yards behind me, and putting spurs to my horse, galloped down the hill towards the two grey objects I had perceived in the distance. "Choo! choo!" shouted François, a cry by which the ostrich-hunters cheer their dogs on, and intimate to them the proximity of game. Past me like lightning the four eager animals rushed, bent on securing the prey which their quick sight had already detected.

The ostriches turned one look on their pursuers, and the next moment they wheeled round, and making for the plain, scudded over the ground at a tremendous pace.

And now, for the first time, I began to experience all the glorious excitement of an ostrich-hunt. My little horse, keen as his rider, took the bit between his teeth, and away we went up and down the hills at a terrific pace. On and on flew the ostriches, closer and closer crept up "Leona," a small, red, half-bred Scotch deerhound, with "Loca," a wiry black lurcher at her heels, who in turn was closely followed by "Apiscuña" and "Sultan." In another moment the little red dog would be alongside the ostriches. Suddenly, however, they twisted right and left respectively, scudding away in opposite directions over the plain, a feint which of course gave them a great advantage, as the dogs in their eagerness shot forward a long way before they were able to stop themselves. By the time they had done so the ostriches had got such a start that, seeing pursuit was useless, we called the dogs back. We were very much disappointed at our failure, and in no very pleasant frame of mind turned our horses' heads in the direction of our camp.

As we rode along we were surprised by the sudden appearance of a man on horseback, galloping towards us. He was dressed in a guanaco robe, and his long black hair floating on the wind, gave him a very wild look. "An Indian!" I exclaimed. But François shook his head, and we rode up to meet the stranger. When he got up to us, he shook hands with François, whom he seemed to know, and, without evincing any sign of curiosity as regarded ourselves, turned his horse round, and prepared to accompany us. I observed that although his face, legs, and hands were almost as copper coloured as those of an Indian, his features were those of a white man. François presently told me that he was a Chilian convict, who had deserted from Sandy Point a good many years ago, and that since then he had lived among the Indians, adopting their dress and customs, till he had now become quite one of them. In reply to my questions, it appeared that he was camping with some Indians on the other side of the lake. They had been out hunting, and he was just returning home when he saw us, and having nothing better to do, thought he might as well pay a visit to our camp.

We were a good deal chaffed when we got home on the score of our non-success, my husband and Mr. B. having had a good day's sport, bringing plenty of guanaco meat back with them. Over pipes and coffee that night a serious council of war was held by the whole of our party, as regards ostrich-hunting for the morrow.

The Chilian suggested the forming of a circle, and professed himself willing, in return for our hospitality, to remain another day and join in the affair. Forming a circle is the method by which the Indians nearly always obtain game. It is formed by lighting fires round a large area of ground into which the different hunters ride from all sides. A complete circle of blazing fires is thus obtained, and any game found therein is pretty sure to become the prey of the dogs, as no ostrich or guanaco will face a fire. Wherever they turn they see before them a column of smoke or are met by dogs and horsemen. Escape becomes almost impossible, and it is not long before they grow bewildered and are captured. In anticipation of a hard day's work on the morrow, we hereupon broke up our council of war, and turned in at an earlier hour than usual.

Next morning, the horses being all ready, we lost no time in springing into the saddle, leaving Storer to take charge of the camp, much to his alarm, and in spite of his earnest remonstrance. The poor man vainly protested that, were the Indians to discover our retreat, he would be perfectly powerless to prevent their pillaging the whole camp, especially as his ignorance of their "jargon," as he scornfully termed the Tehuelche language, would place him in a most helpless position. Regardless of his arguments and imploring looks we rode away, determining to risk the improbable intrusion of the Indians, whose camp lay at least twenty miles distant from our own. For about half an hour we followed Gregorio and the Chilian along a line of broken hillocks, after which, calling a halt, we sent forward Guillaume and I'Aria to commence the first and most distant proceedings of the circle. They departed at a brisk canter, and it was not long before several rising columns of smoke testified that they were already busily engaged. The next to compose the centre circle were my husband, François, and Mr. B., shortly after supported on the right by the Chilian and my brother. Immediately on their left Gregorio and myself commenced operations, and soon a distinct circle of fires might be seen springing quickly up from all points. I could not help being greatly impressed with the novel sight now before me. From the high plain we were on I could look over miles and miles of untrodden desert land, where countless herds of guanaco were roaming in peaceful lazy ease. In the distance towered the peaks of the Andes, wrapped in their cloak of mystery, lonely and unexplored. The huge columns of smoke and the lurid flames of the circle-fires lent a wild appearance to the thrilling scene, to which the frightened knots of guanacos, which were hurrying to escape from the circle and the eager galloping horsemen, lent additional active animation.

For some time, Gregorio and I rode slowly and silently on our way, when a sudden unexpected bound which my horse gave all but unseated me. "Avestruz! Avestruz!" shouted Gregorio and turned his horse with a quick movement. "Choo! choo! Plata!" I cry to the dog who followed at my horse's heels, as a fine male ostrich scudded away towards the hills we had just left with the speed of lightning. Plata has sighted him, and is straining every limb to reach the terrified bird. He is a plucky dog and a fleet one, but it will take him all his time to come alongside that great raking ostrich as he strides away in all the conscious pride of his strength and speed. "We shall lose him!" I cry, half mad with excitement, spurring my horse, who is beginning to gasp and falter as the hill up which we are struggling grows steeper and steeper. But the ostrich suddenly doubles to the left and commences a hurried descent. The cause is soon explained, for in the direction towards which he has been making a great cloud of smoke rises menacingly in his path, and, baulked of the refuge he had hoped to find amidst the hills, the great bird is forced to alter his course, and make swiftly for the plains below. But swiftly as he flies along, so does Plata, who finds a down-hill race much more suited to his splendid shoulders and rare stride. Foot by foot he lessens the distance that separates him from his prey, and gets nearer and nearer to the fast sinking, fast tiring bird. Away we go, helter-skelter down the hill, unchecked and undefeated by the numerous obstacles that obstruct the way. Plata is alongside the ostrich and gathers himself for a spring at the bird's throat. "He has him, he has him!" I shout to Gregorio, who does not reply, but urges his horse on with whip and spur. "Has he got him, though?" Yes—no—the ostrich with a rapid twist has shot some thirty yards ahead of his enemy, and whirling round, makes for the hills once more. And now begins the struggle for victory. The ostrich has decidedly the best of it, for Plata, though he struggles gamely, does not like the uphill work, and at every stride loses ground. There is another fire on the hill above, but it lies too much to the left to attract the bird's attention, who has evidently a safe line of escape in view in that direction. On, on we press; on, on flies the ostrich; bravely and gamely struggles in its wake poor Plata.

"Can he stay?" I cry to Gregorio, who smiles and nods his head. He is right, the dog can stay, for hardly have the words left my lips when, with a tremendous effort, he puts on a spurt, and races up alongside the ostrich. Once more the bird points for the plain; he is beginning to falter, but he is great and strong, and is not beaten yet. It will take all Plata's time and cunning to pull that magnificent bird to the ground, and it will be a long fierce struggle ere the gallant creature yields up his life. Unconscious of anything but the exciting chase before me, I am suddenly disagreeably reminded that there *is* such a thing as caution, and necessity to look where you are going to, for, putting his foot in an unusually deep tuca-tuca hole, my little horse comes with a crash upon his head, and turns completely over on his back, burying me beneath him in a hopeless muddle. Fortunately, beyond a shaking, I am unhurt, and remounting, endeavour to re-join the now somewhat distant chase. The ostrich, Gregorio, and the dog have reached the plain, and as I gallop quickly down the hill I can see that the bird has begun doubling. This is a sure sign of fatigue and shows that the ostrich's strength is beginning to fail him. Nevertheless, it is a matter of no small difficulty for one dog to secure his prey, even at this juncture, as he cannot turn and twist about as rapidly as the ostrich. At each double the bird shoots far ahead of his pursuer and gains a considerable advantage. Away across the plain the two animals fly, whilst I and Gregorio press eagerly in their wake. The excitement grows every moment more intense, and I watch the close struggle going on with the keenest interest. Suddenly the stride of the bird grows slower, his doubles become more frequent, showers of feathers fly in every direction as Plata seizes him by the tail, which comes away in his mouth. In another moment the dog has him by the throat, and for a few minutes nothing can be distinguished but a gray struggling heap. Then Gregorio dashes forward and throws himself off his horse, breaks the bird's neck, and when I arrive upon the scene the struggle is over. The run had lasted for twenty-five minutes.

Our dogs and horses were in a most pitiable state. Poor Plata lay stretched on the ground with his tongue, hot and fiery, lolling out of his mouth, and his sides going at a hundred miles an hour. The horses, with their heads drooped till they almost touched the ground, and their bodies streaming with perspiration, presented a most pitiable sight, and while Gregorio disembowelled and fastened

Patagonian ostrich

the ostrich together, I loosened their girths, and led them to a pool hard by to drink. At length they became more comfortable, and as soon as they seemed in a fit state to go on, Gregorio and I lifted the huge bird on to his horse, and tied it across the animal's withers. Encumbered thus, Gregorio turned to depart in the direction of the camp, followed by Plata, while I went in an opposite direction in search of my companions down in the plain. It was not long before I distinguished in the far distance an ostrich coming straight towards me, closely followed by a dog and two horsemen. Galloping to meet them, I was the means of turning the bird into "Peaché's" jaws, for such was the name of I'Aria's dog. The two horsemen turned out to be the old fellow in question and my brother, who arrived, hot and full of excitement, on the scene just as I was throwing myself from my horse to prevent Peaché from tearing the bird to pieces. Leaving I'Aria to complete the hunter's work, my brother and I rode slowly back towards our camp, discussing the merits of our horses, dogs, and the stamina of the two ostriches we had slain. So engrossed were we that we could hardly believe our eyes when we came suddenly in full view of our snug little retreat, but, nevertheless, we were very glad to dismount and refresh ourselves with the hot coffee which we found old Storer had ready waiting.

One by one the other hunters dropped in. They had all been successful, with the exception of Guillaume; and as we stood grouped round the five large ostriches lying on the ground, we congratulated ourselves on our good fortune, and on the excellent sport we had had. At dinner we passed judgment on ostrich-meat, which we now really tasted for the first time, for what we had obtained from the Indian camp had been dry and unpalatable. We thought it excellent; the breast and wings are particularly good; the latter much resemble pheasant.

CHAPTER X
Indian Law and Equity

After a four days' stay at Laguna Blanca, our horses being sufficiently rested, we resolved to continue our journey. I had got to feel quite at home in the little ravine where our camp had been pitched, and notwithstanding my anxiety to push forward and get over the monotony of the plains as soon as possible, in leaving it felt just a slight touch of regret. Each bush I passed recalled some trivial incident of our stay and came in for a share of the good-bye I inwardly vouchsafed to all my late surroundings.

Whilst we were trotting along, I noticed that one of the brood-mares was continually looking anxiously back, and on counting the foals I found that one was missing. I'Aria, whose attention I drew to this fact, immediately returned to our camp to look for the lost animal, which he thought had probably been left behind in a ravine where the horses had been in the habit of grazing. In the meantime, we rode on, presently passing the site of the camp of the Indians, the smoke of whose fires we had noticed from the Laguna Blanca. They themselves had left it the day before, and were now on the march southwards, as indicated by several columns of smoke which we could see on the distant skyline, it being their habit, when on the march, to light fires at intervals.

Shortly after passing the Indian camp, we were startled by a series of howls, given vent to by Guillaume's dog, "Negro," whom we descried struggling with some animal in the long grass. In a second he was joined by the other dogs, and by the time we got up we found them all engaged in mortal combat with a huge wild-cat, which had already punished Negro most severely, and was defending itself fiercely against the united onslaught of its enemies. Two revolver shots were fired at it without effect, but presently Gregorio managed to kill it with a blow from the "bolas." Up to its last gasp it spat and clawed with undaunted fury, and nearly all the dogs were more or less badly wounded; poor "Negro" in particular, being severely gashed and torn. Whilst we washed the dogs in a pool of water hard by, Gregorio skinned the wild-cat, and then made a search for its companion, which during the fray someone had observed making good its retreat. However, his search was fruitless, and we rode forward again, the incident just related furnishing us with a topic for conversation wherewith to beguile the next hour or so. I'Aria meanwhile re-joined us, but although he had thoroughly searched all the country in the vicinity of our late camp, he had been unable to find any traces of the missing foal, which had doubtless fallen a prey to some puma.

Towards evening we arrived at a large freshwater lake called Laguna Larga, by the shores of which we set up our tents. My husband, going out with his gun, managed to kill an ibis, the first any of us had shot, although we had often tried to do so whilst at Laguna Blanca, being aware that this bird makes excellent soup. This one was put in the pot, and though its meat proved rather tough, the broth it gave was all that could be desired. Laguna Larga, like nearly all the lakes we saw in Patagonia, swarmed with wild-fowl, and amongst other birds we observed two flamingos, whose gorgeous red plumage excited our covetousness, and an elaborate stalking-party was organised with the object of securing one of them. However, they never gave us a chance, and sailed majestically away at the first approach of danger.

Our road the next day lay for the most part along a fertile valley, down the middle of which flowed a narrow but exceedingly deep stream. The breadth of this "cañadon" was about five miles, and we followed its windings for about twenty miles. Its whole length, for it doubtless stretched down to the seacoast, must have been about 150 miles. The grass was tall and green, in many places reaching up to our horses' bellies. As equally fertile valleys are to be found intersecting the barren plains in all directions, an enormous number of cattle and sheep might be reared in this country were it not for the heavy snows in winter and the floods in spring, which latter immerse all these valleys for a considerable period, during which the animals would have to seek sustenance on the plains, where, it is needless to say, they would not find it.

As we emerged from the valley on to the plains, an animal was descried on the skyline, which at first we took for a gigantic guanaco, but which presently resolved itself into a horse. Gregorio having seen it first had become *ipso facto*, in accordance with the unwritten law of the pampas, its owner, that is to say, should it be caught; so, taking I'Aria with him, he rode off to the left, with the intention of getting behind his prospective property and driving it towards our troop. This he accomplished without difficulty. The horse stood staring at our advancing cavalcade for some time, and then came galloping towards us with loud neighs of greeting, spreading consternation among our troop, who neighed and snorted in return, apparently by no means pleased at the sight of the newcomer. Matters were peaceably arranged, however, and after some further slight demonstrations, he was admitted into the troop, evidently much pleased to find himself among his own kind again. According to Gregorio, he had belonged to some Indian, who had probably lost him on the march. I asked Gregorio whether the owner might claim the horse again, and he told me that the law among Indians is that the finder receives about one-third of the value of the object found from the owner. Some difficulty generally arises in these cases as to the value of the find, as the parties naturally overestimate and depreciate it as suits their respective interests; this being especially the case when the bargain is debated between an Indian and a white man. Amongst themselves the Indians are remarkably fair in their dealings, but as they know that the traders cheat them whenever they can, they recognise quite another standard of morality in their dealings with the latter.

As we were approaching the spot where we intended camping, one of the mules, which was heading the troop, suddenly turned and dashed away, and in another instant the whole troop broke up and dispersed, galloping in all directions. What was the cause of this stampede? We pressed quickly forward, but nothing stirred in the long grass, though we scoured everywhere. We were baffled for a minute. "It's a puma somewhere," said Gregorio. The words were hardly out of his mouth when a loud view-holloa rent the air. "There he goes—there he goes!" shouted two or three of our party in chorus, and sure enough, there he was going—a mighty yellow puma—slouching swiftly away at some distance to our left, with my brother following close on his track. For us all to gallop after and come up within ten yards of the puma was the work of a moment, but to get nearer than ten yards or so was quite another matter, as our horses were quivering with fright, and with difficulty were kept from turning tail and bolting from the dread presence of their mortal enemy. Meanwhile the puma, finding himself surrounded, lay sullenly down, eyeing us with dogged hate, and scarcely seeming to heed the presence of the dogs, who were growling furiously at him at a respectful distance from his claws. Finding it useless to try to approach on horseback, my brother dismounted, and a rifle being at hand, took steady aim at the crouching animal and fired. Simultaneous with the report, with outstretched paws and a deep growl, the puma sprang forward, and then fell heavily to the ground, whilst our horses, becoming wholly unmanageable, reared up and fairly bolted. When we again got control of them, nothing would induce them to return to the spot where the now lifeless body of the puma lay, and we had to dismount and walk there. Very fierce and dangerous it looked; and at the sight of its ponderous paws with their sharp talons and its cruel white teeth, we wondered whether, if it knew its own powers, the puma would be such a cowardly animal as it is. They scarcely ever attack man, even when brought to bay, but lie down and doggedly meet their fate, though they can kill a full-grown guanaco with one blow of the paw and pull down a horse with similar ease. The Indians affirm that the puma only bears young ones in two years, but whether this be true or not I do not know. They certainly seem very scarce, comparatively, a circumstance which may be due to this peculiarity, coupled with the fact that the Indians and traders destroy a good number annually.

The excitement attendant on the puma's demise being over, and our horses having been driven together again, we made for our intended camping place. We lodged that night in the valley I have described above, and here, for the first time since we reached the plains, the night was wet. It is by no means agreeable to hear rain pattering down on the canvas of one's tent, especially when one has doubts as to the waterproof capabilities of the canvas, and as yet we had had no opportunity of testing ours. Fortunately, on this occasion the rain did not last long, and, excepting a general sense of dampness, we experienced no further inconvenience. Continuing our journey, on the following day we reached the River Gallegos, which we forded at a spot called "Paso de los Morros;" these Morros being two conically shaped hills of equal height, which form a striking landmark, being conspicuous at a considerable distance. The river at the time was very low; but owing to the inequality of its bed and the rapidity of the current, some care had to be taken in crossing the ford for fear any of the packhorses should come to grief. We passed without any accident, however, and pitched our camp near the bank, under shelter of a snug little clump of beech trees. We liked the place so much that we resolved to pass a couple of days there, especially as the packhorses required a rest after the long march from Laguna Blanca.

The first day we dawdled pleasantly away in all kinds of useful occupations, such as cleaning guns, writing up journals, etc., though I am bound to say that the best part of the time was given up to cooking experiments, my brother and Mr. B. both being anxious to prove their respective superiority in the culinary department. Much amusement was afforded us by a mysterious dish which my brother passed the whole afternoon in elaborating, and which, if his own glowing anticipations had been verified, would certainly have proved a triumph of skill. The care he devoted to the preparation of his dish, and the impressive secrecy with which he conducted his operations, led us into the firm belief that a most agreeable surprise was in store for us. But when dinner-time came, and soup and joint had been hurriedly got through in order to enable us to do all the more justice to his effort, the surprise—for surprise it was—turned out to be a very unpleasant one; the "plat" on which so much care had been bestowed proving to be a homely though curious concoction of rice, preserved milk, and brown sugar, with a decided taste of burn; and after swallowing a few spoonfuls, even its concoctor had to avow, with a grimace, that his exertions had resulted in a failure. My brother having thus signally proved his incapacity for occupying the high office of cook, we for the future left the kitchen department to Francisco's supervision, and very well we fared at his hands.

The next day was spent in ostrich-hunting. We made two or three circles, but game seemed very scarce, and we were unable to entrap a single ostrich. We were going home towards evening, rather disconsolately, when someone observed an ostrich running straight towards us, apparently with the express intention of obliging us, by allowing himself to be killed. But as we started into a gallop to meet him half-way, he changed his mind, and darted off sideways, our whole party following. The dogs unfortunately, as often happens when they are wanted, had fallen behind, and a depression in the plain hid us from their view. It seemed rather a forlorn chase, therefore, as our tired horses were no match for the ostrich, who drew away at every stride. To our surprise, however, he suddenly began to "double," and we saw that he was being hard pressed by one of Guillaume's dogs, from which he had evidently been escaping when he met us. With fresh zest we pushed forward, spreading out in a semicircle, so as to be able to turn the ostrich back to the dog should he double round our way. An exciting chase ensued. The dog, a clever brute, did its utmost to make the ostrich double towards us, but without success, and the speed at which they were both going prevented us from getting any nearer. The dog was tiring, but he held out stoutly, double after double slowly exhausting him. At last, overshooting himself in an attempt to stop short, he turned a complete somersault, and the ostrich, profiting by the moment's respite, literally set all sail and skimmed away, with a strong wind in his favour. "He is lost!" shouted Francisco, reining in. "No, no—the river, the river!" cried Gregorio, spurring the harder, and away we went after him, and right enough, there was the river glittering before us, with the ostrich not fifty yards from the bank, and hurrah! our whole pack of dogs close on his heels. He must take the water, or he is ours. In another second he reaches the bank and pauses. He is in! No—his heart has failed him, and with an ominous droop of his wings, but with a tremendous spurt he has darted off again, with not five yards between him and the straining dogs. On, on we go. The ostrich gains ground; ah, that treacherous bend of the river! It forces him to swerve round, and in a second he is met by Gregorio. A dexterous double rids him of his new enemy, and with a last effort he shoots forward again. But the circle closes, the shouts of the horsemen on all sides bewilder him, he hesitates a second, but in that second the dogs are upon him, and the next he lies a struggling, quivering mass of feathers. Horses, dogs, and men—we are all panting and breathless. The dogs, so hot had been the pace, were too blown to move; and even when Francisco began to cut up the bird, this proceeding, usually of such interest to them on account of the savoury perquisites which fell to their share, scarcely excited their languid attention.

We were rather tired when we got home, and after dinner, the run having been most minutely discussed in all its bearings, we were all glad to get to bed.

CHAPTER XI
Optimism, Pessimism and Bad Luck

The next day found us once more in the saddle, jogging along over the plains with the hopes of a speedy arrival at the Cordilleras to cheer us, under the depression of spirits which the dreary monotony of the country could not fail to produce. The character of the landscape was what we had been accustomed to since leaving Cabo Negro, being in this region, if anything, possibly more barren than usual.

This day's ride was memorable for the immense number of guanacos which covered the plains in all directions. On arriving at a broad depression, we were surprised by the sight of a herd of these animals, which could not have numbered less than five thousand. This enormous living mass defiled past us up the side and over the brow of an escarpment which bound the depression referred to, occupying a space of time of about ten minutes—although they were going at a very quick pace—and once or twice before the day was over, we met an equally numerous herd. How such an extraordinary number of animals can find subsistence on the barren plains, which they even seem to prefer to the grassy ravines, is a matter difficult of explanation. Certain it is that the withered pampa grass must contain great nourishing properties, as the guanacos thrive and grow very fat on it. Although they are generally rather shy, we passed one herd composed of some unusually tame animals. As we approached them, instead of running away, the whole herd came slowly trotting towards us, staring at us with naïve unconcern, which showed that they were innocent of the chase. As it chanced, we had plenty of meat, so we left them unmolested. It was not often that we found them so tame, especially when we happened to be short of meat; in such cases, with the usual perverseness of things, they would scarcely allow one to approach within rifle-range.

As we went on, we observed a column of smoke to the westward, which Gregorio judged to proceed from some fire near the Cordilleras; and from his account it marked the camp of an eccentric Englishman, named Greenwood, who, it appears, particularly affects that region, and who scrupulously avoids contact with his fellow-creatures, scarcely ever coming down to Sandy Point. In fact, according to Gregorio, he seemed to live the life of a hermit. He had renounced the world and its vanities, even to the extent of disdaining the ordinary rough comforts of the other inhabitants of the pampa. Clothed in the most primitive fashion, he roams along the slopes of the Cordilleras, and rather than make a trip to the colony to lay in a store of provisions, passes a whole year on a diet of ostrich and guanaco meat, pure and simple.

I was rather interested in this species of Wild Man of the Woods and kept a sharp look out as we journeyed through that region in the hopes of seeing him. But, if near us at any time—and of course our fires, had he chosen to come, gave sufficient indication of our whereabouts—he did not relax his rule of exclusiveness in our favour, and I, consequently, never had an opportunity of making his acquaintance.

During the march we started up a male ostrich, which had about forty young ones under its care. Though we called our dogs back, nothing could restrain them, and they gave chase, killing one of the small ostriches before we could get up to them; the male bird and the others escaped. The flesh of the young ostrich is not very palatable, so we left the bird, taking only its legs, which make very nice handles for umbrellas and whips. On this day I'Aria again distinguished himself by losing the way, he having been entrusted by the other guides with the leadership on this occasion, as he was supposed to be better acquainted than anyone with this particular region.

For quite two hours we followed him in all directions through an extensive beechwood thicket, in search of the springs we were to camp by that night; and when they were at last found, it was by Gregorio, and in quite another direction than the one in which I'Aria, with his usual pertinacious confidence, was taking us. He came in for a good deal of abuse from his colleagues, and a fair share of black looks from us, all of which he bore with the cheerful indifference which characterised him under all circumstances.

The present was to be our last camp among beeches, as we had now to strike across a perfectly woodless region, on our way to the point at which we intended entering the Cordilleras. These occasional patches of beeches are only to be found in the vicinity of the mountains; in the plains that stretch down to the coast nothing is to be met with in the way of fuel but "berberis" and a few other scrubby kinds of bushes. We therefore made the most of our present abundance of wood, and revelled in huge fires, in order to lay in a store of warm memories at least to carry with us into the bleak region we were about to enter. At dinner this day we tasted a novelty in the way of fowl, of such excellence that I cannot let the occasion pass without expatiating for a moment on its merits. In the daytime we had met with large flights of a bird which the natives call "chorlito," or "batatu," in species something between a golden plover and a woodcock. These birds come down to Patagonia in incredible numbers at this season, to feast on the ripe cranberries which grow everywhere in profusion, and on which the ostriches, ibis, and wild geese all feed and thrive. We had shot some of these "chorlitos," and they had been roasted for dinner on the spit, along with some snipe and wild duck we had brought with us from Gallegos. At dinner, however, they were at first rather neglected, as we had got rather tired of birds, having had so much of them at Laguna Blanca. Presently, however, dinner being finished, some one of our party, in a spirit of careless curiosity rather than from any desire to satisfy an already satiated appetite, pulled one of these chorlitos off the spit, and with a half-deprecating air took a bite of it. But when he had done so, the sudden alteration in his bearing from apathy to activity was a sight to see. The expression on his face, till then one of weary indifference, gave way to a look of intense astonishment, which finally became one of placid delight, as bit by bit the chorlito disappeared down his throat. Though he did not speak, his silent action spoke volumes of eloquent recommendation, and, as may be imagined, we were soon all engaged in eating chorlitos; for a time no sound being heard but the smacking of lips, the crunching of bones, and occasionally such exclamations as "Stunning!" "By Jove!" "Delicious!" etc. etc. The fact is, we had discovered what some Persian king offered half his kingdom for—a new emotion—for so seductively succulent, so exquisitely flavoured, so far beyond anything the gourmet might dream of in the most sublime flight of his imagination, is the flesh of the cranberry-fed chorlito, that the sensation it produces on the palate when tasted for the first time may, without hyperbole, be described as rising to the dignity of an emotion.

Unfortunately, as we travelled northward, we seemed to leave the region of these birds, and only on this and two other occasions were we able to feast upon them.

We witnessed a phenomenon that night in the shape of a moon rainbow, and many were the conjectures as to whether it presaged good or bad weather. Rain is the one thing above all others calculated to make an open-air life unpleasant, and a fear of it being constantly present to our minds, nearly every evening meteorological speculations formed a staple topic of conversation for the whole camp. A great amount of weather wisdom was developed among us, and very soon a party spirit was imported into the question, our camp splitting into two sections—Optimists and Pessimists. Just before bedtime the sky would be conned, and the various weather indications eagerly discussed, often with some heat; and it was amusing to see how frequently the optimists would enlist as arguments in favour of their prophecies of fine weather, the very same phenomena of cloud or temperature on which, on the other hand, the pessimists grounded their equally confident prognostications of rain. On occasions when these discussions had been carried on with more than usual earnestness, should the rain suddenly begin to patter down on the tents in the middle of the night, one might often hear conversations like the following:

Pessimist (in tone of triumph, evidently pleased that it was raining, as his antagonist was thereby confounded). "Well! who was right about the rain? I told you it was sure to come!"

Optimist (cheerily, and half implying that he believes it isn't raining at all). "It is not raining. Well, a drop or two, perhaps, but that's nothing; it will soon be over."

Pessimist (fervently praying that it may rain cats and dogs for the next twelve hours). "You will think it's something though, when you are swamped. (Confidently) It's bound to rain till morning."

Optimist (scornfully). "Rain till morning! Stuff! Why, it never rains long with a full moon" (or no moon, as may suit the case).

Pessimist (derisively). "That's exactly when it does rain. Didn't you know that?"

Optimist (pertinaciously). "Why, only yesterday you said yourself that one might be certain it would not rain long with a full moon, so there!"

Pessimist (conveniently forgetful). "I'm sure I never said anything of the kind."

Optimist gives vent to a sleepy but uncomplimentary ejaculation against people generally who don't know what they are talking about.

Pessimist retorts with drowsy ditto, whereupon follows silence, or silence broken by snores.

On this particular evening the halo was naturally a strong feature in the discussion, and much ingenious special pleading was employed on both sides to prove that its presence was an infallible indication of rain or no rain. This time the optimists gained a signal victory, as the night was fine throughout.

The next day was spent in shooting wild fowl down by a big lake which lay about a couple of miles distant from the camp. I shot a great many lovely specimens of waterfowl, the like of which I had never seen before, and loaded my horse with a great quantity of geese, duck, and plover. Riding home quietly after my day's sport I started up a big ostrich, who rose from the ground not more than a couple of yards distant. How I longed for one of the greyhounds, and shouted loudly to François, whom I could descry in camp idly doing nothing, but he could not or would not hear. Galloping towards him, I hastily explained in which direction the ostrich had disappeared and mounting his horse he went off in pursuit. An hour later he returned empty-handed. He had come across the ostrich and given chase, but the bird, taking to the beech woods, had disappeared therein, closely followed by the dogs. After a long and fruitless search for both, he had been obliged to return without his dogs to the camp. Doubtless, as he observed, they had managed to kill their prey, and were even then indulging in a heavy feed. His words were verified when, later on, the animals returned, presenting an undeniable appearance of having partaken of a large repast. Gregorio had been absent all day in search of guanaco, but as he had gone on foot and taken no dogs with him, he had been unable to secure the one or two which he had managed to wound. So, altogether, our attempts in the chase did not on this occasion flourish.

CHAPTER XII
Features of Patagonian Scenery

After another day's sojourn at this encampment, we resumed our journey. We took a good supply of fuel with us, as we were now entering on the barren, woodless region, during our transit over which we should have to rely solely on the provision we now made.

Leaving the beechwood behind us we rode up on to a plain, on whose edge we could distinguish what appeared to be a little black cloud. In reality it was a peak, or rather clump of peaks of the Cordilleras, at the foot of which we were one day to camp, and towards which for the next few days we directed our horses' heads.

This day's ride, and it was a long one, was by far more monotonous and drearier than any of the preceding ones. The immense plateau over which we rode for six or seven hours was remarkable for its gloom and barrenness, even in a region where all is sterility and dreariness. There was no sun, and the sky, lowering and dark, formed a fit counterpart to the plain, which stretched flatly away to the indistinct horizon, grey, mournful, and silent.

We could not help being affected by the aspect of the scenery around us, and I do not remember ever to have felt anything to equal the depression of spirits to which I, in common with all our party, fell a prey, and to whose influence even the guides succumbed.

For once they drove the troop along without enlivening their work with the customary cheery cries of "Yegua! Yegua! Mula! Mula!" etc., and the very bells of the Madrinas seemed to have a muffled, solemn sound, very unlike their usual lively jingle.

A single incident occurred during that day's march. A little guanaco, which had lost its mother somehow, seeing us coming, instead of running away, trotted trustingly towards us. Unfortunately, our bloodthirsty dogs dashed out and threw it before we could get up to stop them. The poor thing got up again, however, and at first did not seem much hurt. It was the sweetest little creature imaginable, with soft silky fur, and bright, gentle eyes, and it thrust its nose against my cheek in a caressing manner, without the least sign of fear. I determined to carry it with me, in hopes that as it got bigger it would learn to keep with our troop, especially as the mare who had lost her filly at Laguna Blanca would have made an excellent foster-mother for it. But I hardly formed the idea when the little guanaco began to stagger about, and it became evident that it must have received some bite from the dogs which we had not noticed. On examining it this proved to be the case; indeed, in a few minutes its eyes glazed, and to my grief in a very short time it died, apparently without suffering. I would have given anything that it could have lived, as I am sure it would have become attached to me, and finally have found its way to England with us. Tame guanacos are often kept at Sandy Point, and their gentle ways and amiable dispositions make them charming pets.

We were thoroughly tired of our dull march when we at last arrived at a ravine where there were a few pools of water, and where we camped for the night. As we were on short fuel rations, the fire was allowed to go out directly after dinner, and we went to bed, now the only warm place.

Off again the next day, the clump of peaks mentioned above growing more distinct, but still terribly far, and no wood to be got till we reached them. Plains as usual studded with guanacos, but having no time to go out with our rifles, we had to confine ourselves to ostrich meat. Of these birds there was an abundance, and many an exciting run we had pursuing them. Wild-fowl were numerous too, but having eaten every imaginable species—geese, duck, teal, widgeon, snipe, Barbary duck, we were quite tired of them.

After another long march we camped in an open shelter-less ravine, and then again pushed hurriedly on, our stock of fuel getting ominously low, towards the tantalising clump of peaks, which at the end of a long day's ride scarcely seemed to come any nearer. They were now beginning to disappear, as we descended into an immense basin which lay between us and them, and whose farther end was bound by a succession of plateaus, rising abruptly one over the other as it appeared to us, though, when we ultimately came up to them, we found the graduating ascent almost imperceptible.

After camping one night in a most disagreeable sandy region, where our food and clothes and furs all got impregnated with grit and dust, and where we burned our last stick, we again pushed on, with the unpleasant knowledge that that night we should possibly have to camp without a fire to warm ourselves and cook our food. The basin we were now crossing seemed interminable. We were to camp that night at the foot of the escarpment which bound its farther end, whence to the mountains was only one day's march. We were now out of sight of the latter again, but we were cheered by the comforting consciousness that each step was bringing us nearer to them.

Just as it was getting dark, after a weary day's ride, we reached a brawling mountain-stream, which swept along the base of an escarpment, and which we hailed as the first sign that we were at last approaching the Cordilleras. Fording it we pitched our camp in the long green grass, just under shelter of the escarpment. But before unsaddling, eager to see how near we had come to the clump of peaks which had so long been before our eyes, we rode up the escarpment, from the top of which we hoped to get a good view of the country westward.

Our expectations were not disappointed. There, seemingly not a mile away, rose up, compact and dark, not the huddled clump of peaks we had seen two days ago, but a mighty mountain chain, which lost itself westward in the gathering dusk of evening—standing like a mysterious barrier between the strange country we had just crossed and a possibly still stranger country beyond. The sun had long set, and the base of the mountains was wrapped in darkness, but their jagged fantastically shaped crests stood clearly defined against the light which still glimmered in the sky, and here and there a snow-covered peak, higher than its comrades, still retained a faint roseate glow, which contrasted strangely with the grey gloom of all below.

For a long time after complete darkness had fallen over everything, I stood alone, giving myself up to the influence of the emotions the scene described awoke in me, and endeavouring, though vainly, to analyse the feeling which the majestic loneliness of Patagonian scenery always produced in my mind—a feeling which I can only compare—for it would be impossible for me to seize on any definite feature of the many vague sensations which compose it—to those called up by one of Beethoven's grand, severe, yet mysteriously soft sonatas.

I was awakened from my reverie by Francisco, who was wandering about trying to gather a few dry sticks for the fire. Fortunately, he managed to collect enough to enable us to cook a tolerable dinner with; having eaten which, as usual, when we were fireless, we sought our couches as speedily as possible.

The morning broke with every sign of bad weather. The air was heavy and sultry, a hot dry wind blew over the plains, whirling up clouds of fine dust, and the mountain-chain was half-hidden by dark masses of clouds of threatening aspect. We saddled and packed up as hurriedly as possible, fervently hoping that the rain, which sooner or later we saw must come, would kindly hold over till we had reached our destination.

As we journeyed on, the sultriness grew more and more oppressive, and we were vexed by innumerable swarms of minute gnats, which got into our eyes and mouths, buzzed about us in a hopelessly persistent manner, and by no means allayed the state of irritation the combined influence of dust and heat had brought us into. A slight diversion presently occurred by the appearance of an animal whose claims to our polite and immediate attention were not to be denied. This was an enormous puma, who suddenly sprang up from the midst of our cavalcade, sending the mules and luggage horses stampeding away in all directions. True to its cowardly nature, the animal slouched hurriedly off, and disappeared down the side of a ravine. Quick as thought we pursued it, but fast as we galloped, not a trace of it was to be seen. At a short distance from where we stood eagerly searching for the vanished animal, I perceived a small bush growing, the only one for miles round, and to this I pointed as the probable place where the brute had sought a hiding-place. We lost no time in galloping towards the spot, and the terrified snorting of our horses when we drew near, assured us of the correctness of my surmise, and put us on our guard.

We caught sight of him, as he crouched with angry glowing eyes and an expression on his face which, on discovering that none of us carried a rifle, was the reverse of reassuring, especially as we knew from our guides that, for some reason or other, these Cordillera pumas are fiercer than their kindred of the plains, and often attack their assailants,—a piece of temerity the latter have never been known to be capable of.

Fortunately, at this moment, my husband came up with a gun, though indeed it was only loaded with small shot. Dismounting hastily he approached within eight or nine yards of the growling animal. Bang! bang! went his gun, and through the cloud of smoke we saw the puma jump up in the air and fall backwards on the bush. For a moment or two it rolled about in the throes of death, and then, with a last growl stretched itself slowly out, and lay still. Gregorio, who arrived at this moment, set to work at once, to remove its skin. The guides all declared it to be the biggest puma they had ever seen. The skin, which adorns the floor of the room where I am at present writing, measures exactly nine feet from the tip of the tail to the point of the nose. We then hurried on again, anxiously scanning the weather, which meanwhile had grown more and more threatening. The sultriness had increased so as to have become almost unbearable, and the swarms of gnats above alluded to had grown numerous in proportion. Before long a fearful thunderstorm burst over our heads, and for a short time the rain came down in sheets. Then a shift of the wind changed the temperature again. It became quite chilly, and the heavy rain resolved itself into a thick drizzling mist, which soon wetted us to the skin. For hours we rode in this comfortless plight, —wet, cold, and tired, and by no means cheered by the aspect of the country, the little we could see of which—most of it being hidden by the mist aforesaid—looking blacker and sadder than ever.

We were in hopes that at least before evening it would clear up, as the prospect of having to pitch our camp in the drizzling sleet was far from pleasant, but as it grew darker the fog increased in thickness, and soon we could hardly see fifty paces ahead of our horses' noses. How Gregorio managed to find the way, I don't know. At last it being, as near as I could judge, about sunset, we descended a very steep declivity, and came on to what appeared to be a ravine of the ordinary kind, where grass and underwood were apparently abundant. We halted at a semicircle of tall bushes, and set disconsolately to work to get up the tents. This by no means easy task being accomplished, we collected the provisions and cartridges together, and got them under shelter into the smaller of the two tents. Our rugs, furs, and coverings were wet through, so we carried them into the other tent and proceeded to wring them and lay them out to dry. This being done, we turned our attention towards making a fire, but the guides and everybody declared the attempt impossible, and indeed so it seemed, for there was not a dry twig or blade of grass to be found anywhere. Back we all crept into our damp tents and prepared to

The puma's death-spring

dine as genially as we could off sardines and dry biscuit. But though we might choose to resign ourselves thus supinely to discomfort, old I'Aria, for his part, was by no means inclined to do so. Whilst the discussion as to the possibility of making a fire had been carried on, after listening a minute or two to the arguments which were being urged proving conclusively that nothing could be done towards it, he silently withdrew, and busied himself in setting up his own little tent,—a rather dilapidated one by the way, as, whenever he required something wherewith to patch up a rent in his curious garments, he was in the habit of supplying his want by cutting out a piece of the canvas of his "casa" (*house*) as he called it—an ingenious method of robbing Peter to pay Paul.

Meanwhile we had retired to our tents and were beginning to arrange our furs preparatory to going to bed, when I heard some conversation going on between I'Aria, my husband, and Mr. B., the latter an inveterate mate drinker, and who, I must say, had been the only one at the council who had expressed himself hopefully as regarded the possibility of making a fire. Looking out of the tent I saw them all crouched under a bush, dripping wet, but earnestly engaged in some elaborate preparations for conquering damp and getting soaked wood to burn.

Finding they disregarded my friendly advice to save themselves the trouble of doing what could only be termed useless, I withdrew into my tent again. Half an hour later I could still hear them bravely battling against the inevitable, but presently Mr. B. went past my tent with a kettle in his hand. "The fire is burning, is it?" I called out ironically to him. "No, but it will very soon," he replied. "Meanwhile I am going to fill the kettle; would you like tea or coffee?" I answered something sarcastic but sighed. I certainly would have given anything for a cup of hot tea. The hopeful expression of Mr. B.'s face had struck me, so, covering myself up in a cloak, I went up to where I'Aria was busy at work, to see if really there was any hope of his succeeding. I found he had stuck four little stakes in the ground, over which a cloth was drawn, under whose shelter he had built an elaborate structure of wooden matches, laid crosswise one over the other, so as to be handy when required; over these lay a small heap of fine twigs, as dry as could be procured, as well as some stout sticks, and finally several logs, which he informed me would soon be merrily blazing. Everything being ready, he applied a light to the matches, and as soon as they began to blaze, added the twigs, which in their turn, after a little doubtful spluttering, took fire, and presently—this was the critical moment—the sticks were laid on. For a time my worst fears seemed about to be realised, the sticks only smoked viciously, the matches had long burned away, and the twigs now began to glow doubtfully. But old I'Aria did not give in without a struggle. Kneeling down he tried gently to fan the fading glow with his breath. At times, as we anxiously watched it, it seemed to gain strength, at others it became reduced to a single spark. But patience conquered at last; the glow spread, the sticks began to blaze, and before long there was a good blazing fire, which brought every one from his tent, especially as, meantime, the rain had ceased, though a thick mist still hung over everything, making the darkness of the night still more intense. Kettles were put on to boil, maté, tea, coffee, imbibed, and

Francisco prepared an excellent ostrich-fry, *à la minute*, discussing which, blessings were invoked on I'Aria's head,—to his perseverance these comforts being due. Supper over, we groped our way back to our tents, and, enveloped in a dense damp mist, went to sleep, not at all satisfied with the inhospitable greeting the Cordilleras had vouchsafed us.

CHAPTER XIII
A Dilemma

The next morning, I was pleasantly awakened by a bright ray of sunshine, which forced its way through the opening in my tent, leaving me little inclination to sleep any longer. I lost no time in getting up, and stepped out, anxious to see what kind of country we had got into under cover of the fog of the previous day.

For a moment I was quite bewildered by the contrast of the scene now before me and the dreary impression the unfavourable weather conditions had lent to the country on our arrival. I found we were camped in a broad valley, which looked bright and smiling beneath a clear blue sky and a warm sun. A slight breeze swept over the long green grass, which was studded here and there with clumps of calafate bushes, and an enlivening colour variety was given to the verdant carpet by occasional tracts of white and yellow flowers. One end of the valley was bound by some tall hills, covered with dark patches of beech trees, and beyond these again, ridge above ridge, range above range, the snow and glacier covered Cordilleras of the Andes towered majestically to the sky. The air was marvellously clear; looking long westward, I could gradually distinguish, in the haze of the distance, over the mountains which first met my gaze, white snowy ranges, of such height that they seemed to float in mid-air, and only after my vision had acquired sharpness from long concentration, could I trace their outlines basewards. But it was the sight at the near end of the valley which most claimed my attention. From behind the green hills that bound it rose a tall chain of heights, whose jagged peaks were cleft in the most fantastic fashion and fretted and worn by the action of the air and moisture into forms, some bearing the semblance of delicate Gothic spires, others imitating with surprising closeness the bolder outlines of battlemented buttresses and lofty towers. The bare rock which formed them was red porphyry, and the morning sun glittering on it, lent it a variety of bright tints, purple and golden, which were thrown into striking relief by the blue background of the sky and the white masses of snow, which, in parts, clung to the peaks. The abrupt flanks of these tall heights were scored with deep gullies and ravines and strewn with detached boulders of rock; but nowhere was there any trace of vegetation, either bush or grass.

The suddenness with which this novel scenery burst upon me considerably heightened its effect. But yesterday we had stood on the plains, with their eternal monotony of colour and outline; last night we had gone to bed, as we thought, in a similar dreary waste; and now, as if by magic, from the bowels of the earth, a grand and glorious landscape had sprung up around us, as totally different, in its diversity of outline and colour, from that which only a few hours ago had depressed and wearied us, as could well be imagined.

It was amusing to hear the exclamations of surprise with which my companions greeted the scene, as one by one they came out of their tents and gazed on the pleasant metamorphosis which had taken place during our slumbers. We had grumbled a good deal the day before about the country, and had anathematised it with many ill-tempered expletives; but all that was now forgotten, and as we looked around us we felt that our trouble had not been unrewarded.

Taking advantage of the fine weather, we spread our damp furs on the bushes, and, thanks to the wind and sun, they were soon dry. Breakfast over, my brother started off with his rifle to explore the peaks at the end of the valley, whilst we others stretched ourselves on our furs under the shade of some tall bushes, and with the help of books and pipes, a little desultory conversation, and the lazy contemplation of the fair scenery before us, we managed to pass away the hot hours of noon pleasantly enough.

When it got cooler, and we had drunk our fill of idleness, we found plenty to occupy ourselves with. There were guns to be cleaned. I had my journal to write up; and, although I am no good hand with the needle, the rough usage my apparel had lately received made some attempts at sewing and patching imperative. The guides busied themselves in repairing saddle-gear, making reins or lassos from guanaco hide, and similar work. Our English servant Storer, who had somehow created for himself the reputation of one expert in the stuffing of birds and the curing of skins, was busy with several unsavoury smelling specimens of the latter, which he had been carrying about him for some days, having to-day, for the first time, leisure to operate upon them. Mr. B. went off to make a sketch of our camp and its picturesque surroundings, and in searching for a suitable site came across a calafate bush, the blue berries on which were almost ripe. He brought back a capful, and though we found them rather acid, mashed up with plenty of sugar they made a very nice refreshing dish, which was especially welcome to us after our late uniform diet. In the long grass near the stream that flowed down the valley we found some wild celery, which, put in the soup, was a decided improvement on the dried "Julienne" we had brought with us, and of which by this time we had but little left. Just as we were getting rather anxious about him, as it was already near sunset, my brother came back from his excursion to the Porphyry Peaks. Arriving at their base much later than he expected, having been deceived in the distance, he had only had time to climb about half-way up them, but even at that height had got a splendid view of the country beyond, his accounts of which made us eager to penetrate into it as soon as possible. But as our packhorses required rest, this had to be deferred for a couple of days yet.

The next day a hunting-party was organised. Neither our guides nor ourselves knowing whether any game was to be found in the country we were about to enter, it was necessary that we should take a good supply of meat with us. We made a circle in the usual manner, and were successful, as far as ostriches were concerned, inasmuch as, after some good runs, we managed to kill three.

Having observed a herd of guanaco grazing in a valley at some distance, those of us whose horses were still tolerably fresh then set out to try and get one, the meat of three ostriches not being sufficient to last ourselves and dogs for more than two days. The dogs were all too tired with their previous exertions to be of any use to us, so we had to rely solely on our rifles. This being the case, it was necessary to stalk the herd with great precautions, and this we proceeded to do, choosing our ground carefully, so as to keep out of their sight. But we had not gone far when we heard a shrill neigh close by, and looking round, we saw a guanaco standing on the crest of a hill overlooking the valley. He had scarcely uttered his cry when it was repeated at a little distance off by another watchful sentinel, and then they both slowly cantered off, looking back at us as they went along, and neighing loudly at intervals. The herd, meanwhile,

Guanacos on the look out

warned of the approach of danger, leisurely trotted up the escarpment on the other side of the valley, and as leisurely disappeared over the plain. My husband took a vindictive pot-shot at one of the retreating sentinels, but missed him; and we had to make the best of our disappointment, and search for some less watchful herd. In this we had considerable difficulty, the guanacos on this particular day appearing to be shyer than we had ever known them. At last, after a great deal of fruitless stalking, my husband got a shot at a little knot of four or five, who were standing together, almost out of range. One fell, and the others took to their heels. With a cry of triumph, we galloped up to the wounded one, but to our dismay, at our approach, he sprang to his feet and started off full speed after his companions, to all appearance unhurt. Spurring our horses, we followed closely in his wake, down steep ravines, up hills, over the plains, at times losing him altogether, but always catching sight of him again, going as fresh as ever, till at last we began to despair of ever running him down. One by one my companions dropped off, till presently only my husband, Mr. B., and myself, were left in the chase. Had he not been so palpably hit, we should have desisted too; but it seemed a pity, having gone so far, to give in, so we kept on, hoping to tire out our prey by sheer persistence. But gradually, and no wonder, our jaded horses began to show signs of exhaustion; we had run them almost to a standstill, and, reflecting on the distance we had to ride back to the camp, we were just going to rein in, when the guanaco suddenly stopped and lay down. Sure now of getting him, we pushed on towards him. But when we had got to within about six yards of him, up he got, and galloped off again, distancing us at every stride. Hesitating what to do, we kept in his wake, though all the time we were wishing we had never started after him. Slower and slower our panting horses struggled towards a ravine, down the side of which the guanaco had disappeared. We came to its edge and looked down. The guanaco was nowhere to be seen. We were at a loss to imagine what could have become of him. He had not climbed the other side, or we should have seen him emerge on the plain, nor could he have gone along the ravine, either to the right or the left, as we commanded a view of it in both directions for a long distance. In this dilemma we were staring open-mouthed with astonishment about us, when something moved in the long grass below, and directing our steps thither we came upon our guanaco lying stretched out in a pool of blood. The movement that had drawn our attention to him had evidently been his last effort, for he was now quite dead. Examining him, we found the bullet had entered his side, and passing through the lungs and lights, had lodged near the spine; and yet, thus severely wounded, he had gone quite ten miles at a cracking pace! Later on we experienced still more extraordinary instances of the toughness and tenacity of life of these animals, in comparison with whom the cat with its nine lives is absolutely nowhere. Having cut up the guanaco and distributed its meat on the saddles of our horses, we turned back towards our camp; and a long ride we had before we got there. I'Aria, we found, had also killed a guanaco, and we had therefore plenty of meat to last us, should we have difficulty in getting game in the Cordilleras.

The next day was passed in idleness. It was extremely hot, scarcely a breath of wind stirring, and in the evening we were rather bothered by mosquitoes, this being the first acquaintance we made with them in Patagonia. During the day a bird was seen hovering over the camp at an immense height, which we were told was a condor. It was so high up that it looked scarcely bigger than an ordinary hawk. Taking advantage of a moment when it hung perfectly motionless, my husband had a shot at it, and, by a marvellous fluke, the ball took effect, and down the creature came, growing bigger and bigger as it fell, till at last, reaching the earth with a loud thud, there it was, the most gigantic bird I had ever seen. We found it measured twelve feet from wing to wing. The most distinctive feature of the condor is the white down ruff which encircles the neck two or three inches below the head, which latter is completely bare of feathers and repulsively ugly. In the female bird the colour of this ruff is black.

This night the mosquitoes became a positive nuisance. I tried all kinds of stratagems to protect myself from them—such as tying my handkerchief over my face, or burying myself under my furs, but between being smothered and bitten, I preferred the latter evil. Similarly, the plan we adopted of lighting some damp grass in the tent, so as to smoke our trying enemies out, had ultimately to be abandoned in favour of passive endurance of the inevitable. I quite envied old I'Aria. Throughout the night, whilst from all sides exclamations and expletives of varying irritability and force were continually to be heard, the placid snore which floated from his tent showed that, thanks to his parchment skin, he was enabled to bear the sting of the outrageous mosquito with serene indifference.

CHAPTER XIV
Cleopatra's Needles and an Unknown Country

We were up early the next morning, for we had perhaps a long journey before us, the country we were about to penetrate being as unknown to our guides as to ourselves; and no one could say when and where we might find a suitable place for camping that night. All helped to drive up and saddle the horses; their long rest and the rich grass in the valley had done them good, and they were in very fair condition, which was fortunate, as we might have some arduous climbs to face, and pasture lands might be scarce among the mountains.

The day before, the guides had been on a reconnoitring expedition, with the object of finding the most practicable route towards the interior, and having discovered a ravine, which appeared to wind

Ravine entrance to the cordilleras

in the direction of the mountains, and which, at the same time, afforded easy going for our horses, we resolved to make it our highway. Accordingly, all being ready, we said good-bye to the plains, and, fording the stream which flowed down the valley, we entered on the winding ravine, full of curiosity as to what kind of country we were now to break in upon.

The ravine was in itself a fit preparation for something strange and grand. Its steep slopes towered up on either side of us to an immense height; and the sunlight being thus partially excluded, a mysterious gloom reigned below, which, combined with the intense, almost painful silence of the spot, made the scene inexpressibly strange and impressive. Its effect was intensified by the knowledge that since these gigantic solitudes had been fashioned by nature, no human eye had ever beheld them, nor had any human voice ever raised the echoes, which, awakening now for the first time, repeated in sonorous chorus the profane shouts of "Yegua! Yegua!" with which our guides drove the horses along.

We hurried on, anxious to reach the mouth of the ravine, and behold the promised land as soon as possible, but several hours elapsed before we at last reached its farther end, and emerged from its comparative gloom into the sunshine of the open. A glance showed us that we were in a new country. Before us stretched a picturesque plain, covered with soft green turf, and dotted here and there with clumps of beeches, and crossed in all directions by rippling streams. The background was formed by thickly-wooded hills, behind which again towered the Cordilleras,—three tall peaks of a reddish hue, and in shape exact facsimiles of Cleopatra's Needle[1], being a conspicuous feature in the landscape. The calafate bushes here were of a size we had never met on the plains, and were covered with ripe berries, on which hosts of small birds were greedily feasting. The very air seemed balmier and softer than that we had been accustomed to, and instead of the rough winds we had hitherto encountered there was a gentle breeze of just sufficient strength agreeably to temper the heat of the sun. Here and there guanacos were grazing under the shade of a spreading beech tree, and by the indolent manner in which they walked away as we approached, it was easy to see that they had never known what it was to have a dozen fierce dogs and shouting

1. This formation is now called Torres (Towers) del Paine.

horsemen at their heels. But soon we all dismounted round a huge calafate bush, and there we ate our fill of its sweet juicy berries, taking a supply with us to be eaten after dinner, mashed up with sugar, as dessert. Then we gaily cantered on towards the hills, passing many a pleasant-looking nook, and enjoying many a charming glimpse of landscape, doubly delightful after the ugliness of the plains.

Numerous small lagoons, covered with wild fowl of strange and novel appearance, frequently came in our way, and by their shores basked hundreds of the lovely white swans whose species I have already mentioned. Unlike their comrades of the plains, they appeared perfectly tame, merely waddling into the water when we approached close up alongside them, and never once attempting to fly away. I was greatly struck by the thousands of ducks and geese that covered these lakes.

Crossing a broad mountain-stream which ran down from the hills on our left and disappeared into a mighty gorge stretching away into those on our right, we still directed our march along the grassy plain which led direct towards the three huge Cleopatra peaks rising from out of the snow glaciers far ahead of us. The thickly wooded slopes which we could perceive in the distance filled us with eager longing to reach them, as it was many a day since we had last seen trees of any kind. In the vast forests which lay before us we promised ourselves a goodly supply of fuel and many a roaring fire around the camp. On the way we occasionally gave chase to the foxes which started up at our approach. There are a great many of these animals in Patagonia, and one has to be careful to put all leather articles in some safe place at night, or else in the morning one is apt to find them gnawed to pieces by these sly marauders. Their fur is very soft, and silver grey in colour. I resolved to make a collection of their skins and carry them back to England to be made up into rugs and other useful articles. It is very rarely that a dog can catch one of these foxes by himself: our best ostrich hound, "La Plata," after an exciting chase of half an hour, found himself outpaced and outstayed. So quickly can they twist, turn, and double, that it is out of the power of one dog to equal them.

Whilst we were slowly jogging along, my horse, with a snort of terror suddenly swerved violently on one side. Close to him there rose up a magnificent ostrich, who, after one astonished gaze at our party, turned and fled in the direction by which we had just come.

The "Cleopatra needles"

With a merry shout François was after him, followed by my brother and myself. Loca and Leona, who had caught sight of the ostrich in a moment, lost no time in straining every limb to come alongside the fast-fleeting bird, who scudded away at a tremendous pace over the rough, uneven ground. Our progress on horseback was also by no means an easy task, as the line taken by the ostrich presented many obstacles, such as high thick bushes, sharp-pointed, half-hidden rocks, and broad, deep chasms. These latter obstacles could only be negotiated at certain places, as their sides were jagged and rotten; and woe betide the horse who should fall into one of these deep, untempting-looking bottoms. But when his blood is up, and the excitement of the chase at its highest pitch, what keen sportsman cares to crane or wonder what danger lies on the other side of the obstacle that confronts him? His only thought is to get forward and keep a front rank in the merry chase that goes gaily sweeping along. And so on we pressed as fast as we could, and urged our horses to do their utmost. Fully entering into the excitement of the moment, the game little beasts answered willingly to our call, and in spite of the rough, difficult going, we managed to keep the dogs and ostrich in sight.

"They'll soon have him now," calls out my brother to me, as a cloud of feathers float away in the still air, torn from the bird's tail by La Leona, who shakes her head to get rid of those that cling round her mouth and clog her tongue and throat. The bird has begun to double but finds his match in the two clever little ladies at his side, and before long succumbs an easy prey to them both.

This little incident lent a pleasant variety to the winding up of a long tiring day; and full of triumph in the success of our hunt, we trotted towards the camping-place our companions had chosen.

On our arrival we found active preparations going on in the culinary department, and everyone very busily engaged. Three huge fires blazed merrily in front of my tent, and a little farther off a succession of smaller ones indicated the spot where the cooks were employed in preparing dinner. Over one of these hung a pot of soup, carefully superintended by my husband; at another Storer was watching and turning the roasting ribs of a guanaco, while at a third Gregorio occupied himself in frying a rich steak of ostrich, and roasting three or four of their wings as a *bonne bouche*, which was to succeed the roast. Nor were Guillaume or I'Aria idle, as the goodly pile of firewood that lay stacked up near each fire spoke volumes for their activity and energy. After we had unsaddled our horses and turned them loose to join their companions hard by, we refreshed ourselves with mate, and then proceeded to take part in the general work and arrangement of the camp. Mysteriously promising us something extra good in the shape of a new dish, François retired into his tent,

Encampment in the cordilleras

dragging after him the ostrich which we had just killed. The result of his efforts, he assured us, would produce a pleasant surprise, and an agreeable change in the monotony of our daily diet. Though full of curiosity as to what that result might prove, we judged it best to leave him alone, remembering the proverb that "Too many cooks spoil a dish." Collecting the rows of pack-saddles and articles of riding gear, I proceeded to arrange them tidily, together with the numerous sacks and baggage, in a corner of Storer's tent, and then gathering up a roll of guanaco furs, turned my attention to the making up of our beds. On the pampa it had always been a matter of some difficulty to discover ground smooth enough whereon to lay out the beds, on account of the rough, uneven nature of the plains; but on this occasion I had no cause to grumble, for beneath the lofty spreading beech trees the smooth, velvety, mossy turf afforded the softest and most luxurious of feather beds in the world. Our couches were simple enough, as doubtless the reader imagines. The ground supplied the want of a bedstead or mattress, a single blanket occupied the place of a sheet, and our guanaco capas served as covering, being remarkable for their great warmth. With our saddles for our pillows, a complete and final touch was given to the whole arrangement, and on these hard beds, tired with our day's exertions, we would sleep as soundly and comfortably as though they were the most luxurious spring mattresses imaginable.

The beds arranged to my satisfaction, I next proceeded to go the round of the camp to see if everything was in order, on finding which to be the case, with a sigh of relief I felt that my work was over for the day, and the time for rest arrived.

Roughing it may be all very well in theory, but it is not so easy in practice. After a long tiring march, when you have been in the saddle twelve or thirteen hours under a hot sun, it is by no means a light task, on the arrival at your journey's end, to have to unload your horses, pitch your tents, cook your dinner, clean your saddles and bridles, unpack and remove the baggage, and place everything in order and neatness, while it occupies a long and weary time. In England, on your return every day from hunting, you come home tired and weary, no doubt, but it is to a cosy hunting-box, where a warm room, a blazing fire, an easy armchair await you, with servants in plenty to attend to your wants, a refreshing hot bath, and the luxury of a clean change of clothes. But all this is not forthcoming on the pampa, and before you can rest, the whole business I have mentioned has to be gone through, everybody, no matter who it is, taking his or her share of work, while the thought of fatigue must be banished, and every one must put his shoulder to the wheel, and undertake and accomplish his separate task cheerfully and willingly. Only by so doing can things be kept going in the brisk orderly manner they should.

Our camp had been pitched close to the bank of a lovely little mountain stream, which made its appearance from out the thick woods that rose to a great height behind us. The sound of its splashing waters filled me with an irresistible longing for a plunge. Accordingly, armed with a rough towel, I proceeded to follow its winding course upwards, and through the dense foliage of the beech trees I could make out its silver stream descending like a white streak from an immense height. Presently I arrived at a spot where, fed by a small cascade, a clear cool pool of water presented a most convenient and inviting appearance for a bath. I lost no time in undressing and indulging in the luxury of a plunge, which greatly refreshed and invigorated me after the long tiring day I had undergone.

On my return to the camp, I found that dinner was quite ready. Nine hungry human beings, and nine still hungrier dogs, require a good substantial meal. Our *menu* that night was neither mean nor small. As it may interest my readers, I append it:—

Soup.—Guanaco Head, slices of Ostrich, and rice.—Roast ribs of Guanaco.

Fried Ostrich Picane. (Back of the ostrich, resembling a very rich Rumpsteak).

Roast Goose and Ducks.

Ostrich Wings.

Ostrich Liver and fat (consisting of square pieces of ostrich liver and fat, toasted on a stick).

Blood Pudding.

Dessert.—Califatés, Coffee, Maté, Tea, Biscuits.

The blood-pudding proved to be the dish about which François had observed so much secrecy and mystery. It was certainly exceedingly good, and we were loud in praise of its merits. The ostrich liver and fat, a new dish also, was most acceptable, and that night we drank the health of François in a glass of whisky and water all round. Dinner over, we replenished the numerous fires that burned in a semicircle in front of our camp; and then, tired and weary, we sought our couches, and canopied overhead by the rustling trees, with the bright moonlight shining down upon us, slept as sound and contented a sleep as the fatigues we had undergone entitled us to.

CHAPTER XV
Mysteries of the Cordilleras

The first few days of our sojourn in the mountains were spent in making short excursions into the different gorges that stretched away inwards for miles and miles—far as the eye could reach. We were full of curiosity to penetrate and fathom their hidden mysteries; but this was out of the question, owing to the limited supply of provisions which we were able to carry with us. In these solitary wanderings we came across no sign or vestige of the haunts of human beings, and few and far between were the animals that crossed our path. Occasionally, from some jagged plateau or rugged height, we would catch a glimpse of small deer or guanaco, and now and again a wild horse would peer at us suspiciously from behind a huge rock, and then, with a neigh of astonishment rather than fright, dash hurriedly off, its beautiful mane and tail flowing in the breeze, giving it a grand, wild, and picturesque appearance.

Musters tells us in his book "At Home with Patagonians", that the Indians fully believe in the existence of an unknown tribe, or of an enchanted or hidden city, which, they superstitiously believe, lies concealed somewhere in the recesses of these mountains.

Farther north the Araucanian Indians profess to having discovered in their vicinity a settlement of white people who spoke an unknown tongue. Numerous legends and stories are current amongst the Patagonians, who all behold with awe and superstition the distant wooded slopes and far-stretching glaciers of the Cordilleras, into whose shades they never attempt to penetrate.

The Chilotes declare that in the western forests of the Cordillera, an animal exists bearing the form of a wild man covered all over with coarse shaggy hair. Tranco is the appellation by which it goes. It is difficult to bring oneself to believe that amidst these immense solitudes a species of human being does not exist. Imaginative minds may conjure up all sorts of extraordinary fancies, and people unknown regions with strange and fantastic figures; and it is hard to prevent oneself from giving a kind of credence to these vague stories which are told with so much confidence and belief by the inhabitants of the country.

The hilly, undulating country which stretched away in the direction of the three Cleopatra peaks filled us with an eager desire to explore its unknown territory; and accordingly, accompanied by Gregorio and François, we all set off on horseback early one morning, soon after daybreak. The air was keen and invigorating, and we trotted along for some time, following and skirting the line of forest which extended on our right and in front of us as far as we could distinguish. Away on our left stretched a bright green valley, gay with many-coloured flowers, and watered by innumerable streams and watercourses, whilst beyond rose high hills, covered with vegetation, and crowned in the distance by thick impenetrable woods. Calafate bushes, loaded with ripe berries of a great and unusual size, frequently brought us to a halt, as it was impossible to resist their tempting and refreshing aspect.

About midday, when the sun was at its height, and we began to feel the effects of its hot, scorching rays, the valley through which we had been pursuing our way suddenly came to an abrupt termination. Breasting the hill which confined its limits, we halted on the summit to give the horses a few moments' rest, and to contemplate in silence and delight the lovely scene that lay stretched at our feet.

Of a totally different aspect was this new country on which we were entering from that we had just quitted, for the woods closed in on all sides, and huge masses of rocks rose from out their leafy tops, giving the appearance of ruined strongholds to those who beheld them for the first time. Sunny glades, carpeted by rich green grass, opened out here and there, as though they had been cleared and fashioned by the hand of man, while a lovely little stream, which made its appearance from out of the woods on our right, continued its course towards a deep ravine, which we could distinguish in the distance. Away to our left, and surrounded by thick woods, glittered the clear sparkling waters of an immense lake, which we judged to be about two miles distant, and beyond all rose up like a huge frowning barrier, the lofty snow-clad peaks of the Cordillera. Not a sound disturbed the deathlike stillness which reigned over everything; no animal life was stirring, and the impression conveyed to an eyewitness who beheld this scene for the first time was a sense of utter loneliness and desolation.

Descending the hill on which we had halted to breathe the horses, we entered upon the woodland scene I have just described and following the course of the little brook that flowed towards the great ravine, were not long in arriving at the edge of its steep perpendicular descent. It proved to be a ravine of no ordinary size, for many hundreds of feet below, its base was formed by what appeared to be a tiny winding stream, but which a later expedition, of which I have yet to speak, proved in reality to be a broad though shallow river. Far away below us, to our right, roared an enormous cataract, which, half hidden in the trees, left scarcely any part of itself visible, and were it not for the clouds of spray that rose to a great height, an eyewitness could not have distinguished its real position amidst its leafy hiding-place.

We were not long in ascertaining that it would be impossible to get horses down the steep precipitous sides of this great ravine, and therefore reluctantly abandoned any hope of being able that day to make any farther progress towards the three great peaks which still towered in front of us. Directing our horses to the left, we entered a long stretch of narrow woodland, which appeared to lead in the direction of the lake we had distinguished a little time back. It was not

The Wild-horse Glen

long before we struck upon a wild horse track, and concluding that it was formed by these animals on their way to drink at the lake, we followed its tortuous and many winding ways for some time.

Frequently the brushwood became so dense, the trees so close together, that we had to dismount and creep through the openings made by our horses, having previously driven them through. Now and then the path we were following would suddenly cease, and it would be some time before we came upon its track again. At last, we emerged from some thick underwood into a broad clearing, and eagerly pushed forward.

Proceeding at a quicker rate than my companions, I was soon far ahead of them; and in fear of being lost, and anxious to avoid such an unpleasant *contretemps*, I drew rein, and dismounting, sat down to await their arrival. Presently a cracking sound as of sticks breaking close to me attracted my attention. Looking in the direction whence the sound proceeded, I espied a species of deer, of a dark golden colour, eyeing me with extreme astonishment. He was a fine buck, with beautiful branching antlers, and large dark languishing eyes. Close behind him cautiously peered two does, and a little farther off I could make out several other animals of the same kind.

How I longed for a rifle, but of this firearm I knew we had not brought one with us, and though I had a gun, it was not at hand, and was being carried by Storer. Crawling away from the spot as quietly as I could, I placed a good hundred yards between myself and the place from which I had first caught sight of these animals, and then springing to my feet, ran as hard as I could in the direction, I judged my companions were coming. As soon as they came in sight, I endeavoured by signs to get them to halt. They quickly perceived me, and guessing what I wanted, immediately drew rein and waited for me to come up. I lost no time in informing them of the discovery I had made, and taking my gun, proceeded to regain as quietly and stealthily as possible the spot I had lately quitted. The rest of my companions remained stationary, waiting for the report of my gun, which was to bring them all up.

Yes, there he was, a beautiful animal, still in the same attitude of inquiring curiosity in which I had left him. Anxious to avoid spoiling the head, I took aim behind the shoulder, and fired. The report was followed by a crashing sound in the direction in which I had fired. Into the glade some half-dozen deer bounded, and like lightning disappeared into the opposite wood. When the smoke cleared away, I perceived the one at which I had fired on his knees, evidently unable to proceed. Full of anxiety to place the poor beast out of his agony I fired a second barrel at him, which had the effect of knocking him over. Springing up immediately, however, he walked slowly away, seemingly unconcerned and unhurt. I could not make out what was the matter with myself and my gun. He had evidently been hit both times, and yet seemed to be perfectly unconcerned at the whole thing. I could not bring myself to fire again, but Gregorio did with his revolver, and broke the unfortunate animal's leg. Limping away on three, he went and lay down under an overhanging rock, appearing more stupefied than in pain. Disgusted at such butchery, I begged one of my companions, all of whom had come up, to despatch the unfortunate beast, and my husband, going close up to him, placed his revolver within a foot of the deer's forehead and fired. Slowly it sank forward, stunned and apparently lifeless, but when we came alongside it, it was still breathing, and there was no mark to show that the bullet had penetrated the skull. Here François came to our aid, and with the help of his hunting-knife, the poor creature was put out of his misery.

As I wished to keep the skin, the coat of which was very thick and long, Gregorio set to work to remove it. The process occupied some time and proved most difficult and tedious to accomplish. During our stay in the Cordilleras we frequently came across these deer; but our experience of their tameness, the great difficulty of killing them, and the utter absence of sport which lay therein, prevented us from ever again attempting to bring another down. The flesh was decidedly good, and much to be appreciated after the monotonous diet of ostrich and guanaco meat; but even with this inducement at hand, the golden deer of the Cordilleras remained unmolested and sacred in our eyes for the rest of the time we remained in their hitherto undisturbed and peaceful solitudes. If regret could atone for that death, of which I unfortunately was the cause, then it has long ago been forgiven; for, for many a day I was haunted by a sad remorse for the loss of that innocent and trusting life, which had hitherto remained in ignorance of the annihilating propensities of man—that man who, directly he sees something beautiful and rare, becomes filled with the desire to destroy.

The shoulders, ribs, and head were packed on to the horses of Storer, François, and Gregorio, the remainder being left as food for the dogs and condors. Some dozen of the latter, having scented blood, were already hovering high above our heads, and as soon as we were out of sight would doubtless swoop down and make greedy feast on the remains left by the dogs. Five minutes' riding brought us to the shores of the great lagoon towards which we had been directing our steps. Here we dismounted, and tethering our horses, left them to browse on the long rich grass which grew luxuriantly and thickly all round. A couple of hours were quickly and happily whiled away duck shooting. It was not till late that night that we reached our camp in safety, tired and hungry, but having thoroughly enjoyed our day.

CHAPTER XVI
The Struggle Renewed

One evening, after dinner, we were all sitting round the campfire, discussing coffee, when I'Aria, who had gone to have a last look at the horses before turning in, came running back, and announced that he could see the Indians coming down the valley in great numbers. We immediately jumped up and hurried out to inspect the new arrivals, not a little annoyed at the prospect of our privacy being intruded upon by these unwelcome guests.

Looking up the valley, we saw a dark mass moving slowly towards us. Presently it came nearer, and Gregorio, looking at it closely for a moment, said excitedly, "That's not the Indians, but a herd of wild horses; we had better look out for our own!" An extraordinary commotion was indeed visible among our animals. They were running to and fro, evidently in a state of great perturbation, now collecting together in a knot, now dispersing at a gallop over the valley, neighing and whinnying shrilly.

As Gregorio spoke, one of the wild horses detached itself from the main troop and galloped at full speed towards our horses. "Quick! quick! your rifles, or we shall lose our tropilla," shouted Gregorio, in evident alarm; and though we did not quite understand the full extent of our danger, we ran for our rifles, and started off as quick as we could, to get between the wild horses and our own, Gregorio explaining as we ran along, that the wild stallion, if we did not stop him, would drive off our troop, and leave us in the most perilous plight. Of course, nothing more was needed to urge us on to our utmost speed, to avert the threatening danger. But the stallion flew like the wind towards our horses, who were now all huddled together in a corner of the valley, and we could scarcely hope to be in time to save them. Suddenly he staggered and fell; he had got into a bog. In the few seconds he lost in extricating himself we had time to get within range. Bang! bang! bang! went our rifles, but unscathed he sped on, and was soon within twenty yards of our terrified animals, and far in front of us. "We are lost!" cried the guides simultaneously; and filled with dismay, we all stood still, perfectly paralysed at the thought of the position we should be in without horses, three hundred miles away from Sandy Point.

But at this moment Gregorio's big bay stallion, the master of the troop, rushed out to meet the enemy, both halting when they met, and fronting one another. Thankful for this diversion in our favour, we again ran forward, in hopes of being able to get up before Gregorio's stallion should have been compelled to fly, as the superior size of his adversary left no doubt he would ultimately have to do. In the meantime, the two animals, after pawing the air for a second or two, made a dash at one another, and engaged in a fierce combat, carried on chiefly with their teeth, though occasionally they would rise on their hind legs and fight with their fore feet. Our horses, not daring to stir, watched them on one side, and the wild herd, which had meanwhile trotted up close to the field of battle, looked on from the other side, apparently deeply interested in the issue of the struggle.

We hurried along as quick as we could, though, unfortunately, we could make but slow progress, encumbered as we were with our rifles, and retarded by the long grass. Meanwhile—another misfortune—we discovered that beyond three bullets my husband happened to have had in his pocket when we started, and which we had fired off in the first volley, no one had brought any ammunition, this essential having been overlooked in the hurry and excitement of the moment. Hoping we should be able to cope with the stallion, should we get up in time, with our revolvers, we pressed on, our eyes fixed on the two combatants, the endurance of our champion being now our only chance. He was evidently already worsted, and any second might turn tail and fly. Still he fought on, and still we drew nearer and nearer.

Suddenly my brother, who was a little in front of us, seemed to fall. Running to him we found him up to the waist in a bog, which stretched up the valley between us and the horses. It was impossible to cross it; indeed, we had some difficulty in pulling him out. We had to run a good distance before we could get on to firmer ground; and in the meantime the battle went against our stallion, who suddenly turned tail and fled. After giving him a parting kick, the wild horse rushed at our troop, and began to drive them at a gallop towards his own, punishing with vicious bites and kicks any animal that showed signs of becoming refractory, or that did not go quick enough. The moment was critical. We strained every nerve to get between the two troops, as, if they once joined, our chances were hopeless. But for another unexpected diversion in our favour, our efforts would have been defeated. This diversion was the sudden reappearance on the scene of our stallion, who, at the sight of his retreating wives, had evidently once more screwed up his courage to the fighting point.

The combat that now ensued was fiercer even than the last one. Profiting by it, we got up to our horses, who had stood still again, and hurriedly drove them in front of us towards our camp. We had gone some distance when the wild stallion, having again proved victor, came swooping after us, neighing proudly, and evidently meaning mischief. We began to shout and wave our hands as he approached, in the hopes of driving him off. When within forty yards of us, he stopped, but continued to circle round us, stamping and pawing, and neighing angrily. Our object was to drive the horses up to the camp and get to our rifle ammunition, it being evident that the only way to relieve ourselves of this troublesome Don Juan was by despatching him altogether. We soon got near to the camp and shouted to I'Aria to bring us some bullets. At the report of the first shot the stallion fled in dismay, and with such rapidity that the two or three bangs we had at him missed their mark. He made straight for his own troop, who, during the whole performance, had stood in watchful expectation. The moment he reached them they all started off at a gallop, and, in the twinkling of an eye, swept up the steep escarpment on the far side of the valley and disappeared. Our horses were so frightened and bewildered by the day's events, that they seemed to have little desire to graze, but stood quite quiet together for upwards of an hour near the camp. We were in some apprehension lest the stallion should return in the night, but Gregorio said that he thought there was no danger of such an occurrence taking place, and we accordingly turned in and went to sleep, and were glad to see our troop grazing tranquilly next morning as usual.

CHAPTER XVII
Excursion to the Cleopatra Needles

It was arranged that night that Mr. B. and my brother and myself should make an expedition with Gregorio, towards the three strange peaks already mentioned. In order to spare our horses, no cumbersome articles were to be taken, a kettle, some biscuits, coffee, and meat, being all we contemplated carrying with us, except, of course, our guanaco furs and guns.

Thus equipped, we started the next morning shortly after sunrise. Our trip began badly. We had not gone far before my brother got into a morass, out of which he had no little difficulty in extricating himself; and as for his horse, at one time we thought the poor brute would never get out again, so deep had it sunk into the trembling, boggy ground. However, we managed to get it out at last, and, though both well plastered with mud, neither its rider nor itself were any the worse for this little *contretemps*. Proceeding on our journey, we followed Gregorio at a merry trot towards the great ravine, through which flowed that broad and rapid mountain stream, which it was necessary for us to ford.

The ravine side was so steep that we had to dismount and lead our horses down by a narrow track made by the wild horses. This pathway seemed to fall almost perpendicularly down to the river, which roared along, two or three hundred feet below us, and a slip or stumble might have sent us pell mell[1], one over the other, into it. No such mishap occurred, however, and safely reaching the bottom, we proceeded to ford the river. It was not so deep as we had expected, but it ran with great force, and its bed being composed of shifting pebbles and large boulders of rock, our horses floundered and splashed about in a distressing way, and we all got more or less drenched by the

1. A pell mell is a disordered situation.

time we got through it. This being the summer season the water was comparatively low, and we were able to follow the windings of the ravine, riding over the dry strip of river-bed for a good distance. But then the river began to dart about capriciously from one side of the ravine to the other, the consequence being that we were continually finding ourselves obliged to ford it again; and the ravine sides were now so steep and thickly wooded that we had no option but to follow the river. After two hours of splashing, and many a narrow escape from complete duckings, the river made a sudden turn southward, and in order to keep on our road towards the peaks we had to say farewell to our convenient ravine and make our way as best we could through the beechwood forest. This was an arduous task. At times we would get into a thicket which made progress impossible, forcing us to retrace our steps, and try some other route, often to meet only the same difficulty as before. Then a good broad clearing would turn out to be equally impracticable, on account of a belt of bog stretching across it, or a little ravine, which favoured our journey for a time, would resolve itself into an *impasse*, and again we would have to turn back. Fortunately, the weather was fine and sunny, and we made light of our difficulties, occasionally resting for a while to admire some of the many lovely bits of landscape chance presented to our eyes, or to feast on some bush, heavy laden with wild red currants, which were now ripe and sweet. A peculiar phenomenon, suggestive of some great fire in bygone ages, struck me in these forests. Everywhere, among the younger trees, stood huge dead giants, grey and leafless, and partially charred, as if a sudden sea of fire had swept over them, drying up their sap and destroying their vital powers, being quenched, however, by some sudden agency before it had time to destroy their branches and trunks completely. These grey skeletons of a bygone age looked weird and ghastly, standing amid the fresh green trees around them, and the wind, sweeping through their branches, produced a dry harsh rattle, which contrasted strangely with the melodious rustle of the leafy crests of their comrades.

For three or four hours we worked our way through the forest, and I never was more astonished at the marvellous powers of endurance of our horses than on this occasion, to say nothing of their extraordinary cleverness in scrambling over the trunks of fallen trees, and in picking their way through boggy ground, where a wrong step to the right or left would have been disastrous. At last, we reached the outskirts of the wood, all more or less scratched and bruised, and thoroughly tired with our exertions.

But the peaks were still far off, and the sun was getting low, and soon another strip of forest loomed ominously in front of us. We resolved, therefore, to go no farther that day, and accordingly cast about for some suitable camping-place.

We were not long in finding a little nook which was admirably adapted to our purpose. Sheltered by a cluster of moss and grass-covered boulders, and well fenced in by a circle of shrubs and trees, we found a fairy circle of soft, velvety greensward, jewelled here and there with knots of scarlet verbenas and wild violets. Bubbling from out among the rocks a silver clear little stream flowed down its centre, giving just the slight touch of life and movement required to make this sylvan retreat as cheerful as it was cosy, not to speak of its convenience as regards the kettle.

We soon had our horses unsaddled, and then Gregorio and Mr. B. set to work to light a fire, whilst my brother went out with his gun, and I gathered a capful of red currants, which I mashed up with sugar, with a view to dessert. By the time my brother came back, bringing with him a brace of wood-pigeons and parrots, which were soon plucked and spitted, the rib of guanaco Gregorio had set to roast was done to a nicety, and we all fell to and made a hearty meal, finishing with the red currants aforesaid.

Then the men lit their pipes, and the social mate-bowl went round, whilst we lay watching the sun setting over the mountains, gilding their peaks with ever varying tints, and making their snowy glaciers glow warm and golden under its magic touch. Far below, at our feet, lay the ravine, with the river we had so often crossed that day, looking like a winding silver thread in the distance. Around us reigned perfect peace; the chattering flocks of parrots, which had made the woods noisy during daytime, had gone to their leafy roosts, and not a breath of wind stirred the silent trees. A few little birds, who no doubt had their homes in the chinks of the boulders which formed the background of our camp, hovered around us anxiously for some time, till, finding they had nothing to fear from their strange visitors, they took heart, and hopped from stone to stone into their respective lodgings, and, after chirping a note or two, were silent for the night.

We were not long in following their example, and rolling myself up in my guanaco robe, with my head on my saddle, I slept as sound and sweet a sleep "under the greenwood tree" as ever blessed a weary mortal. Neither Puck nor Ariel played any pranks with me; though, for ought I know, Titania and Oberon, and their fairy following, flying from the sceptical modern spirit which ignores them, may well have made these secluded sylvan haunts their own.

We were in the saddle early the next morning, and, plunging into the woods, pursued our way through the same difficulties which had hampered our progress the day before. After a time, however, we came to a region evidently much frequented by wild horses, and eventually we hit on a path worn by them right through the woods, and following this, we jogged along at a very fair pace. Soon our horses began to neigh and prick up their ears as we advanced towards a clearing. Their cries were answered from somewhere beyond us, and pushing forward into the open, we came upon a herd of wild horses, who, hearing our advance, had stopped grazing, and now they stood collected in a knot together, snorting and stamping, and staring at us in evident amazement. One of their number came boldly trotting out to meet us, and evidently with no pacific intentions; his wicked eye, and his white teeth, which he had bared fiercely, looked by no means reassuring. But suddenly he stopped short, looked at us for a moment, and then, with a wild snort, dashed madly away, followed by the whole herd. They disappeared like lightning over the brow of a deep ravine, to emerge again on our view after a couple of seconds, scampering like goats up its opposite side, which rose almost perpendicular to a height of six or seven hundred feet. They reached its crest at full gallop in the twinkling of an eye, and without pausing an instant disappeared again, leaving us wondering and amazed at their marvellous agility. I had often seen their paths leading up hill-sides which a man could scarcely climb, but till now that I had witnessed a specimen of their powers with my own eyes, I had scarcely been able to believe them possessed of a nimbleness and cleverness of foot which would not discredit a chamois.

From the open space on which we were now standing we could see a broad lake lying at the base of some very high hills, behind which lay the mighty mountain which culminated in the three peaks we were desirous of reaching, and as a ravine appeared to wind in that direction from the head of the lake, we now pushed forward towards the latter, occasionally profiting by numerous wild horse paths to expedite our advance. After a weary scramble of several hours' duration, we threaded a last belt of forest, blundered and floundered through a last bog, and after a short ride over a grassy plain studded with bushes, which were literally blue with a profusion of calafate-berries, found ourselves on the shores of a splendid sheet of water. The sight well repaid us for our trouble. The lake, which was two or three miles broad, lay encircled by tall hills, covered with thick vegetation, which grew close down to the water's edge. Beyond the hills rose the three red peaks and the Cordilleras. Their white glaciers, with the white clouds resting on them, were all mirrored to marvellous perfection in the motionless lake, whose crystal waters were of the most extraordinarily brilliant blue I have ever beheld. Round the lake ran a narrow strip of white sand, and exactly in its centre stood a little green island with a clump of beeches growing on it. Each colour—the white, the green, the blue—was so brilliant; the scene—the wooded hills, the glaciers rising into the blue above, and sinking mirrored into the blue below—was so unique, the spirit of silence and solitude which lay over all so impressive, that for a long time we stood as if spellbound, none of us uttering a word. Suddenly we were startled by a rushing sound behind us, and in another instant, making the air shake as it went, and almost touching me with the tip of its mighty wing, a condor swept past us, rising with rapid flight up, up, up into the air, we following him with our eyes, till he became a mere speck on the sky, and finally disappeared, thousands of feet up in the air. This incident seemed to break the charm that held us silent, and we broke into a chorus of exclamations of praise and wonder as every second some new beauty in the scene before us struck our admiring gaze. Resuming our journey, we rode along the narrow strip of beach towards the head of the lake. Occasionally we were forced into the water, as at some spots there was no beach at all; but at any rate we got on much quicker here than we had up to the present, and in a comparatively short space of time found ourselves at the head of the lake. We were close to the three peaks, which we could now see were parts of the crater of an extinct volcano—the other portions of which had fallen in, a prey to the action of the weather. We camped by the side of a little stream which flowed into the lake. All night long we could hear the thunder of avalanches, or what, perhaps, might have been the rumbling of some distant volcano; and I found myself nervously expecting a repetition of the earthquake which had surprised us so disagreeably at the Laguna Blanca.

"We were the first who ever burst on to that silent sea"

In the morning we rode up a tall hill, from which we could get a good view of the interior. At the same time, we were able to assure ourselves that it would be useless, slightly provisioned as we were, to attempt to penetrate any farther, the country before us being still more thickly wooded than that we had already traversed.

For some distance we could catch glimpses among the hills of bright green valleys, with whose excellent pastures our nimble friends the wild horses were doubtless well acquainted; and farther on rose a forest of white peaks, one towering above the other, till the tallest faded, hazy and indistinct, into the skies. I would fain have dived into their farthest mystery, but it was not to be; so, with a sigh of regret, we turned our horses' heads in a homeward direction. We got back to the camp late in the evening, having taxed our horses' powers to the utmost to accomplish our return trip in one day. Our account of the wonderful blue lake and the strange country beyond excited the envy of those who had remained behind and led to a discussion as to the practicability of our entering the mountains, bag and baggage. But the difficulties in our way were too many and formidable, and reluctantly we were compelled to abandon this seductive plan.

CHAPTER XVIII
Good Bye to the Cordilleras

A few more days spent in the Cordilleras brought us near the time when it was necessary to begin to think of returning to Sandy Point. Our provisions were beginning to sink rapidly; tea and coffee and sugar we still had plenty of, but the biscuit bags were getting ominously low, and all our other dainties had already been consumed; and many of our camps were painfully remembered in connection with this or that article of food, which had been partaken of there for the last time. Thus, near "Los Baguales" we had finished our last tin of butter; "Los Morros" witnessed the broaching of our last tin of preserved milk; and here, in the Cordilleras, we ruefully swallowed our last dish of porridge. Guanaco meat is good, so is ostrich meat; good, too, is an open-air, gipsy life in a bright climate, with lots of sport and pleasant companionship; but the goodness of all these things is materially enhanced by the accompaniment of good cheer, and materially depreciated by the lack of it. Thus, when our daily *menu* began to consist of a series of ingenious changes on the monotonous theme of ostrich and guanaco meat, varied only by baked biscuits, our thoughts somehow began to run in the groove of home; and we often found ourselves talking of "dear old England" and its roast beef in a strain of affectionate longing. Somehow the air of Patagonia did not seem so bracing and inspiriting as at first; we began to grow sceptical on the subject of guanaco and ostrich hunting; we discovered that the wild duck was too tame to give real good sport, and that snipe-shooting in a country where these birds get up in flocks, is simply a matter of loading and pulling the trigger. Discomforts and hardships, of which we once made light, we now began to take as serious matters, and our tempers, once so sweet and accommodating, had begun to grow acrid and touchy. We all felt more inclined to dwell on the weight of our individual opinions, and less disposed to value those of our companions. Once we had avoided discussions, as liable to disturb the harmony which reigned among us; now we welcomed them as pleasant irritants, and even went out of our way to provoke them. The result was that one day, on somebody's suggesting that perhaps we had better think of returning; after a little opposition, as a matter of course (for in our then mood it was quite sufficient for anybody to propose a plan for everybody else to immediately gainsay it), we unanimously agreed that, considering that we had seen a good deal of Patagonia, considering, too, that our provisions were nearly exhausted, and that our horses were very stale, it was better to start at once.

So one morning the packhorses were driven up, and the familiar occupation of loading them gone through. It had now become a much simpler matter than formerly, and we were enabled to comfort ourselves with the reflection that the loss in our larder was a gain as regards the time economised every day in packing up.

Before leaving our pretty camp we carved our names on one of the trees, and erected a cairn, on the top of which we left a bottle—the only emblem of civilisation we could spare. Then, mounting, we turned our backs on the Cordilleras, and set out towards the ravine we had entered by, whose name, among the traders, is "The Wild Horse Ravine." As we were riding along, a solitary horse suddenly appeared on the crest of a hill, and, after eyeing us for a moment, came tearing down towards us at a frantic gallop, with a loud neigh, and perhaps dangerous intentions. Our troop of horses scattered in all directions; Gregorio and I'Aria got out their "bolas," prepared for emergencies, and we curiously awaited the sequel of the incident. Nearer and nearer came the untamed steed, without abating his speed one jot, and evidently determined to charge right at us. We began to feel uncomfortable, but put our trust in Gregorio's deftness, though it was perhaps well it was not put to the test. When within about ten yards of us the wild horse suddenly stopped, stood still for one second, and then turned, and, with two sets of "bolas" whizzing harmlessly round his ears, went bounding away as fast as he had come, never stopping till he reached the top of the hill he had first appeared on. This was the last we saw of the "Baguales."

Late in the afternoon we crossed the ravine where we had camped before entering the Cordilleras. Here we were assailed by a thick cloud of mosquitoes, who annoyed us and our poor horses horribly, buzzing round us, and biting viciously wherever they could settle. For a time nothing was to be heard but angry exclamations and objurgations, mingled with occasional cries of fiendish joy as one of us succeeded in destroying half a dozen of our thirsty tormentors with one slap of the hand. But from the fury of their numbers there was no refuge, opposition only increased their virulence, and those who were fiercest and most energetic in driving them off were always surrounded by the thickest cloud. Relief only came when we got out of the ravine into the plain, and there one puff of wind swept our enemy clean away in a second, not one mosquito remaining to curse at or to kill.

Thankful for our release from this annoyance, we were not disposed to grumble very much at the oppressive heat to which we were exposed during the whole of the day, though the sun beat down on us from a cloudless sky with overpowering force, and our burnt and blistered faces smarted painfully under its fiery rays. We camped that night near a broad lagoon, and for the next few days continued our journey over the plains, without anything of note occurring. Hitherto we had been pretty fortunate as regards the weather, and the nights especially, with hardly an exception, had been calm and fine. But one march before reaching Coy-Inlet River we camped in a broad valley, where our experience of Patagonian nights was unpleasantly varied. Shortly after we had gone to bed, the misgivings which the threatening aspect of the sky had called up, as we took a last glance at the weather before turning in, were more than realised. The wind began to pipe ominously through the grass, and before long it was blowing a regular gale. A sudden squall carried our tents clean out of their pickets and sent them whirling through the air. A scene of the most uncomfortable confusion ensued. It was pouring with rain, pitch dark, and the wind was blowing with such force that it was hard to keep one's legs. Rugs, and clothes, and smouldering embers were being blown in all directions; everybody was blundering about in the darkness, tripping up over something, or falling against someone else; and the howling of the wind, the rush of the river, the chorus of loud imprecations in various languages, and the unearthly moaning and whimpering of the dogs, made up as wild a scene of noisy confusion as could possibly be imagined.

Several vain attempts were made to set up the tents, but the wind was too strong; and at last, perfectly drenched through, we had to give up the attempt, and crawl into whatever furs first came to hand, to wait till the storm should pass over. This it did not do till about four o'clock in the morning, just as it was getting light. It was too late or early to go to bed again then, so we crept out, sleepy, and damp, and miserable, and drank hot coffee round a smoking fire, till the sun got up and warmed us thoroughly.

We were to camp that evening by the Coy-Inlet River, and as it was a good way off we set out soon after breakfast. We passed several herds of guanaco, and also a herd of about eighty or a hundred ostriches. I had never seen so many together before. We gave chase to them, but the dogs got so excited, running first after one ostrich and then after another, that at last they all got away. A calamity happened to us that afternoon. The mare who carried the two little bags with all that remained of our greatest treasure—our biscuits, suddenly took fright at something, and galloped wildly away. We followed her course with anxious eyes and beating hearts, not daring to go after her, lest it should aggravate her fears. For a time the pack sat firmly, and we began to breathe, but even while we watched, oh, horror! it began to incline towards one side, and then gradually slid over. The moment the mare felt it underneath her she began to kick out, and galloping quicker and quicker, in a very few seconds she was packless and pacified. Then only did we gallop forward to know the worst, and the worst was bad indeed. A long trail of broken biscuits, sown in the grass, marked the course the unfortunate mare had taken, and when we got to the bags only a few small handfuls remained. We tried to gather together what we could, but the biscuit, by long travel, had broken into fine dust, and it was quite impossible to pick much out of the long grass it had fallen into. Our last kettle had also severely suffered in the fracâs, a big hole appearing in its side when, after a long search, it was at last found. Guillaume talked hopefully of being able to mend it, but failing this desirable consummation, farewell the cheering cup of mate; farewell the morning bowl of grateful coffee; farewell content—the camp-life's chiefest comfort gone! Slowly and mournfully, we tied up what was left of the biscuits in a small canvas bag, which Gregorio secured to his saddle, and then, after having devoted a quarter of an hour to grazing on all fours on such fragments as could be found among the grass, we continued our journey, reflecting on the vanity of all things.

We arrived at Coy-Inlet River that evening, and fording it, camped near the bank. It rained again during the night, but as there was little or no wind, it did not matter much, and excepting a pervading sense of dampness, we suffered no great discomfort. Continuing our march that day over the plains that lay between Coy-Inlet River and the Gallegos, we saw the smoke of numerous fires in the distance; but there was no response to the fires we lit in answer, and so we concluded that they were only old fires, which were still smouldering. The next day one of our party had an opportunity of practically testing the value of fires as a means of signalling one's whereabouts in the pampa. He had got up early in the morning and had gone out on foot at about five o'clock with his rifle, to try and stalk a guanaco. At ten o'clock he had not returned. As we had only a short march to make that day, it did not matter if we started a little later than usual, so we lay about, waiting for his return. Eleven, twelve o'clock came, but still no signs of him. He had now been away more than seven hours, and I began to think that something must have happened to him. We therefore rode up on the plains to look for him, lighting fires at intervals, to show the position of the camp, and anxiously scanning the horizon to see whether he had also made a fire. But though we rode about for a long time nothing was to be seen, and we went back to the camp, wondering what could have happened. Just as we were in the middle of a perplexed discussion as to what steps to take in the matter, to our relief he suddenly came into the camp, blood-stained and tired, and carrying the head and ribs of a guanaco on his back. Shortly after leaving the camp he had wounded a guanaco, which went off, however, and led him a long dance for two or three hours, without his being able to come within range of it again. In despair, he at last fired a couple of shots at it from a long range, but, as it seemed, without reaching his mark. These shots exhausted his ammunition, our supply of ball-cartridges being very low, and he having only allowed himself three rounds. Loath to abandon the wounded animal, he had followed it pertinaciously over ravines and hills, always vowing to himself that beyond a certain point he would follow no farther, but always being lured on by the signs of exhaustion the guanaco was showing, to go just a little farther. At last he had the satisfaction of seeing it lie down, and with a shout of triumph ran forward to despatch it with his hunting-knife. But at his approach the guanaco jumped up again, and slowly as it ran, it was enabled to outdistance its relentless pursuer, who was already thoroughly done up with his exertions; but feeling that with patience he must conquer at last, he felt less inclined than ever to abandon his prey. Already numerous hawks and condors were circling over the doomed guanaco, and the thought that the fruit of his labours would only go to provide a feast for these hateful marauders was an additional incentive to persevere. At last success rewarded his efforts. Waiting till the guanaco lay down once more, he approached it by degrees, and then, when within twenty yards or so of it, made a dash towards it. It stumbled in trying to get up, and he had just time to rush up and catch it by the ear, and with a happy stroke of his long hunting-knife end its sufferings. It was only when he had cut it up, and laden himself with the best parts, that he began to reflect that in the excitement of the chase he had quite forgotten in which direction the camp lay. He had followed the guanaco now to the right, now to the left, often having to run to keep it in view, and all he knew was that several hours must have elapsed since he started in its pursuit. He lit several fires, but he only had a few matches, and the fires unfortunately soon went out, so that he had no means of showing us his own whereabouts. However, he struck out in a direction in which he imagined the camp must lie, and kept wearily trudging on under his load, which, tired as he was, he was naturally loath to part from. After he had gone a good distance he looked around, and then the skyline behind him appeared to be singularly like that he remembered having seen on leaving the camp. But then the skyline to the left, somehow, had the same look too. Which was the right one? He was just revolving this puzzling question in his mind, in no very pleasant humour, when he caught a glimpse of the smoke of the fires we had lit, and happily not far off, in the direction he had instinctively chosen from the first as the right one. The sight gave him new vigour, and though he had still a good distance to go, he managed to reach the camp at last, without having to throw away the meat which had cost him such a hard day's work.

CHAPTER XIX
An Unsavoury Meal

We rode down a broad valley, which led to the Gallegos River, where we were to camp for the night. On reaching its farther end we were suddenly surprised by the sight of an Indian camp, composed of three tents, which were pitched on the other side of the river. Having little curiosity to make the acquaintance of their inmates, we continued our journey along the river towards our intended camp, but Gregorio and Mr. B. rode over to see them. They re-joined us an hour afterwards; Mr. B. had found an old friend, an Argentine Gaucho, named Isidoro, who had accompanied him on a former trip, and whom, curiously enough, he had parted from a year before, on exactly the same spot where he now met him. I was glad to hear that Isidoro was going to pay us a visit the next day, as I had heard a great deal about him, and was anxious to make his acquaintance. We camped near the river, seven or eight miles away from the Indian camp, and consequently, we hoped, rather too far to attract a call from these people, the disagreeable experience of their visit whilst we were at Cape Gregorio being still fresh in my mind.

Early in the morning we saw a man riding in the direction of the camp, who, I was told, was Isidoro. He presently appeared among us, and, except for his moustache and beard, and the superior cleanliness of his dress, he might have been taken for an Indian. He was warmly welcomed by the guides, amongst whom his unequalled proficiency in all that pertains to the pampa craft, and his personal character, had gained him great prestige. Isidoro did not stop long, as he was going to hunt with the Indians that day; so, after having taken a few cups of mate, and smoked a pipe or two in silence, he said good-bye, and took his departure.

As he rode away, I could not help admiring his manly bearing and his perfect seat on a splendid, well-bred looking horse, which seemed not unworthy of its master. He wore his guanaco capa with a certain foppish grace that one might have looked in vain for in Gregorio or any of the others, and every article of his accoutrements, from his carefully coiled lasso to the bright-coloured garters round his new potro-boots, was perfectly finished and natty.

After he had gone, my husband and myself started off guanaco-hunting. We soon killed a guanaco and were busily engaged in the laborious operation of cutting it up, when we heard a grunt, and looking up, saw an Indian behind us on horseback. He watched our clumsy efforts for some time in silence, occasionally breaking out into loud laughter, and then dismounting, took out his own knife, and with a few adroit and easy cuts, did the whole trick in no time. He rewarded himself for his labours by cutting out the kidneys and the heart, and eating them raw and bloody, there and then! This disgusting repast over, he smacked his lips, mounted his horse, and rode away, grinning eloquently, and leaving us wondering and horrified.

The evening after our halt at Gallegos we camped in a stony, rocky region, where there was very little grass, but plenty of quail, several of which we shot, though we found them to be very dry and unpalatable. It poured all the next day, so we were compelled to remain where we were, much against our will. To have to lie all day in a little tent, with a dreary bit of grey landscape to look out upon, while the rain patters on the canvas in a remorseless, dispiriting monotone, is one of the most severe trials one's patience can be put to, and ours came very badly out of the ordeal, Patagonia being by no means complimentarily alluded to in the course of these weary hours. However, towards sundown, it cleared up, and we were able to have a turn and stretch our limbs in the open air before it got dark.

Two days after leaving this camp we struck the Indian trail to Sandy Point, and on the third we camped opposite Cape Gregorio, not far from the place whence we had made our visit to the Indians. Here we intended halting for a couple of days to take in a good supply of meat before starting for Sandy Point, as neither guanaco nor ostriches were to be met with, except by a mere chance, any farther south, and all our other provisions being exhausted, we had now to rely solely upon the product of the chase for our food.

In the morning two traders passed through our camp, and we were delighted to find that they had a small bag of bread, which they were taking to the Indians. They sold us twenty small loaves, each about the size of a penny roll, for five pounds; and I think they got the best of the bargain, for the bread was half mildewed and scarcely eatable, and so heavy, that even the stomach of an ostrich could scarcely have compassed its digestion with impunity. Famished as we were, we preferred to give it to the dogs, who showed their good sense by turning up their noses at it; and unless the foxes rashly experimented upon it after our departure, for aught I know these expensive loaves may still be lying in a fossil state on the Patagonian pampas!

We all went out guanaco-hunting that day but were not very successful. I'Aria managed to run down a young one with his dog, and Mr. B. shot one; but as he killed it some twenty miles away from our camp, he could only bring the head and the two sides, not daring to load his dead-beat horse with more.

But meat had to be procured somehow, so next day, whilst the others went on along the trail with the packhorses, my husband, Mr. B., myself, and Gregorio, went out hunting again, intending to catch up the others before the evening. We rode for several hours towards Cape Gregorio, but although we saw several ostriches, they got up very wild, and pursuit of them was always out of the question. Guanaco, there were none to be seen. This was very dispiriting; if we did not manage to kill anything here it was still more unlikely that we should be able to do so farther on. Our companions were relying on our efforts, and to have to join them empty-handed would have been in itself vexatious enough from a sportsman's point of view, apart from the serious and practical consideration that we could scarcely go on to Sandy Point, which was quite three days' march away, without food. So we kept riding on towards Cape Gregorio, in the hopes of still being able to find something. We presently sighted some guanacos grazing at the base of a ridge of hills, and whilst Gregorio went after an ostrich, which sprang up at that moment, we three spurred our horses, and separating, so as to attract as little attention as possible, rode towards them.

I soon lost sight of my companions, who disappeared down some of the many gulches that led to the valley where guanacos were grazing. Fervently praying that one of us might be successful, I hurried on. When I got into the valley, to my chagrin I saw that the guanaco, already aware of danger, were moving slowly up the valley, not at a great distance from where I was, but still a good way beyond rifle-range. Mr. B., who was a long way to the left, was much nearer to them, and my husband was in a similar position to the right. As we approached, the guanaco trotted up among the hills and disappeared. We had no option but to follow them, entering on the range of hills at different points, as the herd would probably scatter as soon as we came close upon them.

I came upon them of a sudden, and, as I had surmised, they all broke into different directions. I took a flying shot at one, but missed, and presently a report on each side of me showed that the others had had a shot too. I was soon joined by my husband, who had also been unsuccessful, but Mr. B. did not turn up, and we began to hope that he might have killed something. We presently saw him galloping full speed up a distant hill after a guanaco, which was no doubt wounded, but which seemed to be going too gamely to admit of our being very sanguine as to his chance of ultimately getting at it. We waited for some time, but he did not reappear, and so we went down into the valley to look for Gregorio. He soon came in sight, and, unfortunately, as empty-handed as we ourselves were. Matters were now getting serious. The day was far gone, and to catch up our companions on our jaded horses would have been a hard task, unless we started at once. We were therefore obliged to relinquish all hope of getting any guanaco ourselves that day, our only consolation being that Mr. B.'s prolonged absence boded that he at least had been successful.

We waited for him a little, but as he did not come, knowing that he could find the way to the place where the others were to camp, we rode on, lighting fires at intervals, to show our whereabouts. Our horses were so tired that we could scarcely get them into a trot, and to our dismay we suddenly found it was getting dark. The sky had been clouded all day, and we had had no sun to judge the time by, the result being that we were two or three hours out in our calculations. It is very easy to guess the time within half an hour or so, under ordinary circumstances, but the excitement of our various runs after guanacos and ostriches had so absorbed us that the hours had slipped by unperceived. We thus found ourselves face to face with the uncomfortable knowledge that, it being quite impossible to catch up the others, we should have to go to bed in the open, and unless Mr. B. had killed his guanaco, supperless. The unpleasantness of this at any time disagreeable contingency was increased on this occasion by the prospect of our getting wet through into the bargain, for the aspect of the sky was very threatening, and it was only in keeping with our day's luck that there should be a downpour of rain during the night. But there was absolutely nothing to be done but give in to the inevitable as cheerfully as we could, so we dismounted and unsaddled our horses, carefully tethering them to some bushes, lest they should stray away in the night, and then we sat down to await Mr. B's coming, the numerous fires we had lit on the way making us quite sure he would be able to find us. But it grew darker and darker, the tooth of hunger got fiercer and fiercer, and still he did not come. What could have happened? Surely he must have run down the guanaco, or given up the chase hours ago. Perhaps he has met with some accident! That's impossible! With these and other reflections we beguiled the anxious moments, hoping against hope that before long a goodly rib of guanaco would be roasting at the blazing fire we had prepared in rash anticipation of its advent. But time went on; already we could scarcely distinguish the bushes in the distance, the hills faded away altogether into the darkness, and our missing companion did not come. Having strained our eyes blind, peering into the gloom, we now sat silently, straining our ears to catch the slightest sign of an approaching footstep; but our hopes grew gradually fainter and fainter, and at last we were obliged to give them up altogether. Gregorio fortunately found a small piece of guanaco meat in one of his saddlebags, which we cooked and ate, a small mouthful being all each of us got. Mingled with our regrets for our enforced fast were speculations as to what Mr. B. was doing at that moment. Had he killed his guanaco, and (horrible thought!) was he at that very moment perhaps roasting its head in the ashes? or was he in a worse plight than ourselves,—supperless as well as companionless? Our thoughts reverted to the other party too, who no doubt were in some anxiety as to what could have become of us. I did not sleep very sound that night, nor did my companions, as may be imagined. Just as day broke the dogs gave tongue; there was a crashing among the bushes, and Mr. B. rode up, with an eager, hungry look on his face, which boded no good. "Have you got anything to eat?" were his first words, to which our despairing answer was, "Good gracious! haven't you?" And our faces grew longer and more disconsolate than ever, as the hopes of a good breakfast, which had hitherto sustained us, were remorselessly shattered on both sides.

There was nothing to be done but immediately saddle and ride off to join our companions. On the way Mr. B. told us how he had followed the wounded guanaco till he had run his horse to a complete standstill, and like us, having been overtaken by darkness, had been obliged to stop where he was till morning.

After several hours' ride we got to the place where the others were camped and found them very much alarmed at our protracted absence, though they had naturally supposed that we had been taken a long distance out of our way by the chase. We lost no time in making a hearty meal on what remained of the guanaco meat, which being finished, there was no food of any kind in the camp.

CHAPTER XX
The Mystery Solved

We had a short march to make next day, and it was nearly noon, therefore, when I'Aria started off on his usual morning task of driving up the horses.

In the evening, as one may rely on their not straying very far, the horses are turned loose, after being unsaddled. In fact, no other method would be practicable, for if they were kept picketed during the night they would not be able to graze, and would soon become useless. As they all follow the bell-mare, one is always sure of finding them together, even should they stray three or four miles in the night, which, although it does occasionally occur, is quite exceptional. That, however, this necessity of leaving the horses at liberty may give rise to considerable inconvenience, and possibly bring one into the most serious dilemmas, we had an opportunity of discovering at the cost of some anxiety and a day's hard labour.

After I'Aria had been gone about an hour we began to wonder at his prolonged absence; but as there had been a strong breeze during the night, it was very probable, as Gregorio suggested, that the horses had wandered some distance in search of a sheltered valley. But another hour elapsed, and still I'Aria did not appear. Guillaume and François then went off in different directions to continue the search, agreeing to light a fire should either of them sight the horses.

We in the meantime were left a prey to very disagreeable reflections, though as yet we had no strong grounds for fearing the worst. We kept an anxious watch for the first signs of smoke, especially in the direction I'Aria had taken, as he must have covered five or six miles by the time he had been gone. To our dismay he presently turned up, however, very tired and footsore, without having seen a trace of the horses anywhere. Matters now began to look really serious, but we still comforted ourselves with the hope that François or

Guillaume would be more successful. But they too, after a time, came back, bringing the same dismal story. The situation looked gloomy; a hundred suppositions were hazarded as to what could have become of the horses. I'Aria said he had "cut the trail" on the side he had taken without success, and Guillaume and François having done the same, it was clear that the only direction in which the horses could have gone was over the plain at the back of our camp, though what could have induced them to leave the pasturage of the valley for the barren upland it was hard to understand. Meanwhile there was nothing to be done but immediately make search for them in that direction, though our prospects of finding them seemed small indeed. Should we not do so we should have to accomplish the rest of our journey to Sandy Point on foot. We had eaten our last round of guanaco meat that morning, so that a four days' walk on empty stomachs, apart from being an unpleasant undertaking, was one which it was a question whether our powers were equal to compassing. We might, it is true, opportunely meet some trader on the way, from whom we might obtain provisions; but, on the other hand, we might not be so fortunate; and, on the principle that it never rains but it pours, we were justified in considering the latter contingency as the probable one. We commenced our task, therefore, with feelings the reverse of cheerful. Leaving Storer in the camp, we all went on to the plain, and started off in different directions towards the distant hills that bound it. A fire, should any of us be successful, was to immediately communicate the news to the others.

With my eyes bent on the ground, eagerly scanning it for any trace of a hoof mark, I walked slowly along, occasionally giving a glance over the plain, in the hopes of seeing the welcome column of smoke rise up into the air. But time went on, and my hopes of success grew fainter and fainter. Gregorio had expressed a fear that the horses had got on to the Indian trail to Sandy Point; and taking to it, had gone off at a trot towards Cabo Negro, on whose pastures they were "at home," or "aquerenciado," as the natives say. The possibility of their having done so assumed more and more the feature of a probability, as hour after hour passed, and I was still only half-way across the plain, and no traces of the objects of my search as yet forthcoming. In fact, it seemed useless to continue plodding on farther, and instinctively I broke off, and turned to the left, observing that there the plain ended in a hilly country, where, although I'Aria had assured us he had searched in that direction, it certainly seemed more likely that the horses would be, supposing they had not gone to Sandy Point. It was a happy inspiration of mine; I had not gone half a dozen yards down a grassy ravine before, turning a sharp bend, I suddenly came upon the whole troop, quietly grazing at their ease, in supreme indifference as to the trouble and anxiety they had caused half a dozen human beings for the last five or six hours. My first step was to throw a few lighted matches into the long dry grass, which I left to do their work, and then, by dint of some patience and cunning, I managed to persuade one of the tamest horses to allow me to get my arm round its neck and effect its capture. Improvising a kind of bridle from my scarf, I mounted, and driving the horses together, conveyed them towards the camp, not a little proud and elated at my achievement, which was due rather to good fortune than judgment, for, had I followed out the plan of search we had agreed upon, who knows what the upshot would have been? Meanwhile, the matches had had due effect; fanned by the breeze, the fire spread quickly, and soon the ravine was ablaze across its whole breadth, a mighty column of smoke being whirled high into the air, carrying, doubtless, intense relief into the hearts of my companions, who were still toiling over the plains.

I soon got to the camp with my charges and was thankful to be able to lie down and rest after my exertions. One by one the others dropped in, and, as may be imagined, we were all equally elated at so fortunate an issue of a *contretemps*, which might have had the most serious consequences,—just on the eve too, of the conclusion of a trip otherwise particularly free from dangerous mishaps.

It was too late to set out that afternoon, so we passed the remainder of the day in trying to shoot some duck for supper. In the pleasure of finding our horses again, we were not disposed to grumble at minor hardships, and cheerfully, therefore, we endeavoured to make as good a supper off a brace of small duck, which was all we could kill, as eight hungry people might be expected to do.

After a cup of coffee next morning, we drew our belts a little tighter, and set out, keeping a sharp look-out, on the forlorn chance of an ostrich coming within coursing distance. But during the whole of that day's march neither beast nor fowl, save a fox or two, showed itself, and as our appetites, which we had kept in tolerable subjection during daytime, began loudly to assert themselves towards sundown, the spirit which reigned among us was by no means a cheerful one. We were just discussing the faint probability that existed of our meeting an Indian trader before reaching the Colony, when suddenly we descried a man riding along the trail towards us and driving two horses before him. With a unanimous shout of delight, we all galloped forward to meet this welcome stranger, on whose provisions we meant to make a friendly but extensive raid. But, to our astonishment, on perceiving us, he suddenly drew up his horse, hesitated for a moment, and then dashed away over the pampa. Without stopping to inquire what could be the motive of such extraordinary behaviour and seeing only that our chance of supper was vanishing as fast as four legs could carry it, we all clapped spurs to our steeds, and galloped after him with as much alacrity as he had shown. The harder we went, the more he urged his horse along, occasionally looking back in a state of evident terror. For five minutes or so this strange man-chase continued, neither pursued nor pursuers gaining any ground on one another, but then we gradually drew nearer to our quarry, whose horse was already beginning to show signs of distress. We were soon within earshot, and called loudly on him to stop, saying that we were friends. Whether he heard us or not I don't know, but the effect of our shouting was that he redoubled his efforts, and for a time the chase again became doubtful.

But we were not to be beat; curiosity to know this man's motives for running away from us as if we were wild beasts, combined with an equally strong desire to obtain some provisions from the amply filled saddlebags which were gliding along in front of us, kept us to our work, and we felt that till our horses dropped this queer quarry must be followed. The spurt he had put on soon died away, and then we crept up to him again, wild with excitement, and giving vent to some sounding "view-holloas," which, now I come to think of it, may have possibly increased the terrors of the poor man's situation. But everything comes to an end, even a stern chase, and soon Gregorio was within ten or twelve yards of the unknown. "Párese amigo, soy Gregorio," he called out several times, and at last, feeling G.'s hand on his shoulder, the man did stop. In a second or two we were all up, more or less breathless with the run. The man, with whom Gregorio was now rapidly conversing in Spanish, looked very pale and frightened at first, but gradually the expression on his face brightened as he listened to Gregorio's explanations, and eventually he even began to smile. We, meanwhile, eager to know the solution of the mystery, pressed Gregorio to solve it. It appeared that this man was a convict, who had escaped from Sandy Point two days before, and having "requisitioned" two Government horses, was now on his way to the Santa Cruz river, on the other side of which he would be free from pursuit. When he saw us coming towards him at a gallop, he had been seized with a sudden panic, thinking we might want to capture him, and had galloped off, with the results known.

Of course, we could not ask for any of his provisions as he would require them much more than we should; so, after exchanging a few words with him, we left him, and proceeded to re-join Storer, who had remained behind with the horses whilst we had been engaged on our novel hunt.

The incident furnished us with matter for conversation for a time, but it was not long before we came back to the more important topic of food, for we were now all of us really faint with hunger, and our prospects of getting anything for the next thirty-six hours were faint indeed.

Our goal that evening was the "Cabeza del Mar," an arm of the sea which runs for some distance inland, and which, at a certain point, is fordable at low water if the wind is not blowing strongly from an unfavourable direction. As we rode along, we caught a glimpse of the sea itself—a welcome sight, and forgetting our hunger for a moment we gave a loud cheer.

At about seven o'clock, just as it was getting dark, we arrived at the "Cabeza del Mar." We found that we should not be able to ford it for four or five hours; and as we were anxious to get to Cabo Negro as soon as possible, in order to break our prolonged fast, we decided on passing that night, rather than wait till next morning. Having relieved the packhorses of their loads we sat down by the fire and brewed some coffee with the last spoonfuls that remained to us of that comfort, and having drunk it, nothing remained for us but to wait and dream of the meal we meant to devour on the first opportunity.

We tried to snatch a nap, but few of us succeeded in doing so, as hunger kept us awake, and so the hours dragged their slow length wearily along, whilst we sat and waited for the tide to serve. To add to the discomforts of our plight, the sky covered over and the rain began to fall, and the night got so dark that we almost thought we should not be able to cross over. However, the time came when we thought the tide ought to serve, and we rode down to the water to inspect matters. Occasionally a moonbeam breaking through the thick rainclouds allowed us to get a glimpse of the rocks in the middle of the water; and our guides were thus able to judge the right moment for making the attempt. There was, as they said, just the possibility of the water not being quite low enough to enable us to cross without more or less of a ducking, and besides, in the darkness, the leader might mistake the way, and a false step would land us into a rocky bottom, where we might flounder hopelessly about, and in all probability get unhorsed, and God knows what besides.

These considerations served to make us feel rather uncomfortable when the moment arrived for us to commit ourselves to the chances that might be awaiting us in the dark mass of water which swept eddying swiftly past us, and but for the acute pangs of hunger we should certainly have deferred the experiment until daytime. But no time was to be lost, so, ranging in single file behind I'Aria, who was acting as guide, we started—the other horses, with Guillaume and Gregorio driving them, following. For a few seconds there was a great deal of splashing and shouting, incidental on the objections shown by the packhorses to take the water; but soon they were all in and fairly on their way. Then came a few seconds' silence, as we drew into deep water, every one cautiously following his leader, so as to be able to rein in in time should the latter come to grief. Suddenly I'Aria gave a cry, and through the darkness we could dimly see him floundering about, his horse having evidently lost footing. After splashing about for some seconds, however, he got all right again, and calling out to us to keep more to the left, he moved on. The water was now up to our knees, and at each step it got deeper, but fortunately our horses still kept their footing, and soon the worst was over, and the bank was reached without any mishap having occurred.

All the dogs had remained on the other side, crying and yelling in a gloomy concert, as they saw us leaving them behind; but as soon as they saw us ride up on to the plain, they plunged into the water, and swam over in no time.

After having counted the horses and examined their packs, which had all got well drenched, as we ourselves had, we continued our ride, with the intention of marching the whole night, so as to arrive at Cabo Negro in the morning, for we were now positively frantic with hunger. For a time, notwithstanding the intense darkness, we managed to get along pretty well, but presently we found that we had got off the trail somehow, and we had to stop, whilst the guides blundered about in the darkness, searching for it. Then, after we had got on to it once more, the horses shied at a big white stone lying on the road, and bolted in all directions, and of course had to be got together again—a task which involved nearly an hour's delay.

Apart from these mishaps, our progress was necessarily so slow, owing to the darkness, that we at last came to the conclusion that after all it would be better to halt where we were, and proceed at daybreak. Acting on this determination, we immediately unsaddled, and, too tired to put up the tents, rolled ourselves up in our furs, and slept, or tried to sleep, till morning. I think this was the most unpleasant night of the whole trip. Faint with hunger, drenched and cold, I could not get repose, although I felt as tired and jaded as could possibly be. The ground too, where we were camped, was stony and hillocky; and when, at the first sign of dawn, I crept out of my furs, my bones were so stiff that I could with difficulty move, my companions being all in an equally bad plight. But we were in good spirits for all that. Four hours' riding would bring us to the wood of Cabo Negro, and there we should get food in abundance. Never had the horses been so quickly saddled and packed as on that morning; within half an hour from commencing operations we were already cantering along the trail.

Scaling the brow of a steep hill we came in view of the familiar landscape—the Straits and the Cordilleras, and not far off the black patches of beechwood round Cabo Negro; and, nestling amid them, the little farmhouse on whose stores we projected a determined raid.

My brother and Mr. B. now rode ahead in order to have something ready against our arrival. After two- or three-hours' sharp riding they reached the farm-house, and without speaking a word rushed off to the kitchen, and laid their hands on and utterly devoured what was to have been the breakfast of the farmer and his family. The farmer appeared on the scene just as they had swallowed the last mouthful, and it appears being no doubt used to such strange visits, seemed less surprised than one would have imagined to see two dirty wild-looking men sitting uninvited in his kitchen, who between them had calmly demolished the morning meal of a whole household.

Having thus satisfied their own immediate wants they applied themselves to catering for ours; and to such good purpose that, by the time we reached our old camp under the beeches of Cabo Negro, we found a good fire already blazing, half a sheep hanging on a tree, ready for roasting, and such stores of bread, eggs, and other provisions as made our eyes glisten and our mouths water. How we feasted need not be told. I think very little of that half sheep remained to be warmed up for supper, and most of the other provisions shared a similar speedy fate.

CHAPTER XXI
Civilisation Again

We had still three days to wait till the date for the arrival of the steamer, and as we by no means liked the idea of having to pass them in Sandy Point, we resolved to remain at Cabo Negro for a couple of days more, and only get into the colony in time to settle with our guides, and make ourselves look a little civilised against going on board.

But as we were naturally most anxious to get our correspondence, my brother rode into Sandy Point to fetch it. He returned, bringing a bagful of letters and newspapers, and we devoted a whole afternoon to their perusal, and to discussing their contents. These letters seemed to bring us back to the world again, to the world and its almost forgotten responsibilities, pains, and pleasures, which but the day before had seemed as remote to us as if we had quitted the earth altogether and were living in some other planet. How many things seemed to have happened since we had been away, and how the interest in these events was magnified, hearing of them as we did, thousands of miles away from home, after so long an absence! Occurrences which, in the bustle and noise of ordinary existence, would hardly have excited more than few exclamations of surprise, or scarcely a passing thought, now seemed to assume the most important proportions, and were discussed at inordinate length, and with the keenest interest. There was a letter from the gamekeeper, telling with interminable prosiness how cleverly he had surprised, in flagrante delicto, the man whom he had long and so wisely suspected of poaching; how, notwithstanding every care on his part, the severe winter had proved too much for a favourite old setter; and, thanks to his efforts, how extraordinary a number of pheasants there was in the copses, etc. Another from the head stable-man, with intelligence of a similar nature from his department; lengthy documents from the agent, telling how one tenant couldn't pay his rent, how another wouldn't though he could, how one lot of cottages required repairing, and how advantageous to the property, if a fresh lot were built; the peculiarity of all these epistles being the predominance of the bad over the good news. Then were letters telling how A. had married, and "the very last woman one would have thought, too;" how B. had got a divorce, "and no wonder, one might have seen that all along;" how C. had gone off to shoot big game in the Rocky Mountains; and how D. had merely gone and shot himself—and so forth, and so forth; every trivial item affording us a goodly space for lengthy gossip, a luxury which, since our departure for the plains, had so signally failed us. It is only when unable to indulge in it that we find what an important factor the tittle-tattle and small talk of ordinary life is, in general conversation.

There were several papers too in our budget, and we devoured their three-months' old intelligence with no less avidity and eagerness than that with which we had perused our letters.

That day passed, and the next, and then the hour came for us to saddle up once more, and ride into Sandy Point. As may be imagined, this time we did not jog along behind the pack-horses. Leaving these to the care of the guides, to come on at their leisure, we cantered merrily on alone—along the familiar path by the shore of the Straits. As the huts of Sandy Point came in sight, we began to realise that at last we were getting back to civilisation, and prospectively to England, and already plans of what we were to do on arriving home were formed and discussed. There was only one night more to pass before setting foot on board the steamer which was to take us back to the world; but so impatient were we, that even that short time seemed all too long, and we wondered if it ever would pass.

Soon we were trotting along the streets of Sandy Point; and, reaching Pedro's house, dismounted, and found ourselves under a roof once more! Pedro, advised of our coming, had prepared breakfast for us, and, without more ado, we sat down to it. We handled our knives and forks very awkwardly at first; it required almost an effort to eat in a civilised manner, and, accustomed of late to take our meals in a recumbent position, we by no means felt very comfortable in our chairs. And now, for the first time, the scales fell from our eyes, and the sight of the clean tablecloth and neat room caused us to become aware of our own personal appearance, and the enviable "giftie" was ours, of seeing ourselves as others saw us. The sight was certainly not a delectable one. Our looks and garments were not out of keeping with our late life in the pampas, but surrounded by cleanliness and civilisation, they were decidedly out of place. We had performed our ablutions as often and as thoroughly as circumstances would permit, but they had not permitted much. The men of our party, particularly, were unpleasant to look at. Their hair had grown long and elfin; their faces were tanned to a dark red brown, which the dust, and the smoke from the camp-fires had deepened into—well—black; and their unshaven chins were disfigured by a profuse growth of coarse stubble. Our clothes did not bear close inspection, the blood of many a guanaco, the grease of many an ostrich-dinner, the thorn of many a calafate bush, had left their marks; and, altogether, a more ruffianly, disreputable lot than we looked it would be hard to imagine. But hot water, soap, and razors, and a change of raiment, did wonders; and when, after several hours' hard work, we met again we were scarcely able to recognise one another.

We passed the day in settling with the guides, and in packing up our few traps in anticipation of the arrival of the steamer early next morning.

Feeling tired, I went to sleep early, but the comfort I expected from lying between sheets again was by no means vouchsafed me, and the soft mattress and cool sheets, instead of inviting slumber, seemed to frighten it away. I felt half inclined to get up and go to sleep on the floor. However, my eyes closed at last; and from a dream, in which I was once more chasing the ostrich in sight of the memorable Cleopatra Peaks, I was awakened by Mr. Dunsmuir banging at my door, telling me that the steamer had arrived and that it was time to be off. I jumped up and dressed hurriedly, and found all the others ready to go on board. The luggage had already been put into a boat, and there was nothing further to be done but to say good-bye to our guides and walk down to the jetty to embark.

I had only one regret on leaving Sandy Point. The day we arrived at Cabo Negro one of our dogs, called "Pucho," who was rather a favourite of mine, and whom I wished to take with me to England, was suddenly missing. Pucho, a peculiar dog, had joined us under peculiar circumstances at our camp at Laguna Larga. We were quietly sitting round the campfire after dinner, when suddenly the dogs jumped up and began to bark furiously at some unseen enemy.

Pucho

We got up and peered out into the dusk, but could see nothing, though it was evident that something there was, for the growls of our dogs increased in earnestness and fury every instant. "A puma!" suggested somebody, but our horses were grazing quietly, so it could not be a puma. "An Indian, or some trader, perhaps!" was another equally unfounded surmise. What could it be? Here, as if to settle the mystery at once, the dogs all rushed out of one accord, and for a few moments we could hear a terrible snarling and growling going on in the distance. It came nearer and nearer, and then the cause of the commotion was explained. Surrounded by our dogs, who were giving it a by no means friendly welcome, a strange dog walked slowly towards the campfire. It bore its tail between its legs, seeming half-humbly, half-defiantly, to crave admission into our circle. Its humble demeanour, however, only bore reference to *us*, for the defiant manner in which it occasionally bared its white teeth and turned on our dogs whenever they came too near, showed that it cared little for them. We called out in friendly tones, and this settled its bearing for once and for all. It turned round, made one savage dash at one or two of its tormentors, and then calmly made its way towards the fire, looked out for the most comfortable spot, stretched itself leisurely, and lay down with its head resting on its crossed paws, seemingly as much at home as if it had known us all its life. I ventured to stroke it, but my advances were received in a most unfriendly, and, considering its position of alien outcast, audaciously impertinent manner, for it snapped viciously at me. But from the first "Pucho," as we called him, made it a point of distinctly refusing to be patronised. He joined us, he gave us to understand, not on sufferance, not as a suppliant for our favours, not as a guest even, but as an equal; and this status he claimed as regards us only, for as to our dogs, he ignored them completely, though willing, as subsequently appeared, to make use of their good services. He looked sleek and fat, a circumstance which led us to think highly of his powers of speed, as it is by no means easy for a dog to run down a guanaco singly, and most dogs who lose their master, as this dog had evidently done, soon die of starvation. We therefore congratulated ourselves on his arrival, as we hoped he would be able to afford our own dogs help in the chase. But we had grievously reckoned without our host. The next day, on the march, a guanaco was sighted close to us. Now was the time. "Choo! choo! Pucho!" we shouted, expecting to see him speed out like an arrow after the guanaco. But nothing could have been further from his thoughts. He looked first at us and then at the guanaco for a moment, not without interest, perhaps, but certainly without showing the slightest inclination to hostile demonstration. Then, with another look at us, which said as plainly as words could, "Well, that's a guanaco, no doubt, but what then?" he quietly trotted on. We were very angry at seeing our hopes deceived, besides being surprised at his extraordinary demeanour; but Gregorio, giving the dog the benefit of the doubt, said that perhaps it had only been trained to run ostriches, as Indians frequently teach their dogs to do. This seemed plausible enough, and our confidence in Pucho was momentarily restored. Presently an ostrich started up. Now then: "Choo! choo! Pucho!" was the excited cry again. All the other dogs flew out like the wind after the bird, and Pucho followed them. But only at a trot, and apparently merely to judge how the other dogs behaved, for he soon stopped, and contented himself with watching the chase till it disappeared from view, and then he leisurely came back to his usual post at my horse's heels. Everybody was enraged with him; Francisco suggested that being a "bouche inutile," Pucho should be knocked on the head with the bolas; but I could not hear of this, and Pucho's life was spared. And so he remained with us, and I had ample opportunities for studying his peculiar character. As on the first day, so he continued. Although generally there or thereabouts when a distribution of the spoils took place, he never once helped the dogs in the chase. That this did not arise from inability or want of speed, but rather from a sense of his own superior dignity, was shown by the fact of his once having been seen to pursue and catch a fox, a feat none of our other dogs were capable of. Amongst other peculiarities he had a way of mysteriously disappearing if the day's march was too long. "Where is Pucho?" was a frequent cry, and "Thank God, he's gone at last!" was an ejaculation often heard on these occasions. But so sure as the guanaco-rib for dinner was done to a turn, the soup ready, and the fire blazing comfortably, so sure would Pucho suddenly appear on the scene, look out for the cosiest spot near the fire, and cheerfully await his supper, as if nothing had happened.

When, therefore, he was missing at Cabo Negro, I took little notice, thinking he would be sure to turn up. But dinnertime came, and no Pucho; nor did he appear again, even when we went on to Sandy Point.

This was the thought that was troubling me as I walked down to the pier, for I had taken a liking to this dog, or I had better say I held him in reverential awe; for I think he would object himself to the term "like," as savouring of patronage. Half absently, therefore, before going down the ladder into the boat, I turned round to take a last look for Pucho. Surely that is a dog coming down the street, I thought, as I looked up; and right enough it was a dog, and what is more, Pucho himself! There was no mistaking the calm mien, the leisurely trot. He picked his way along the battered pier, half wagged his tail as he saw me—a great condescension, and then, without a moment's hesitation, led the way down the ladder into the boat, much to the surprise of my companions, who had thought and hoped that they had really seen the last of him.

I took him, or rather he came to England *with* me, and as I write this he is sitting in the cosiest corner by my fire, a privilege he allows my pet terrier to share with him, an act very foreign to his usual nature, and one for which I have never been able to account.

So here we are on board at last. We say good-bye to Mr. Dunsmuir, the anchor is weighed, the screw goes round, and we are off. Sandy Point disappears from view; one by one Cape Negro and Cape Gregorio are passed, and before I know it—so engrossed am I in the thoughts that crowd into my mind at the sight of these well-known points—we are abreast of Cape Virgins. It fades again astern, there is no land on either side, and Patagonia, bleak and silent and solemn, with the days we spent on its mysterious shores, is behind us.

As I write, these days come vividly to my mind again, and in fancy I once more behold that distant desert land,—the land of the lonely plains, where the guanaco and the ostrich and the Red Indians roam far from the ken of mankind, and where I spent a careless, happy time, which I can never forget. I remember the days when, after a long and weary ride, I slept, pillowed on my saddle, the open sky above me, a sounder and sweeter sleep than I had ever slept before; I remember those grand mountain-scenes, where we traced the wild horse to his home, through beechwood glens, by lonely lakes, by mountain torrents, where no mortal foot had ever trod before me. I remember many an exciting chase and many a pleasant evening spent round the cheery campfire. I remember, too, many a discomfort—the earthquake, the drenching rains, the scorching sun, the pitiless mosquitoes, and the terrible blasting winds. But from the pleasure with which I look back on my wild-life in Patagonia, these unpleasant memories can detract but little. Taking it all in all, it was a very happy time, and a time on whose like I would gladly look again.

THE END

Lady Florence Dixie in 1895

Other books by EDICIONES HISTÓRICAS
available in digital stores:

Este libro se terminó de imprimir
en el mes de diciembre de 2024
en DP Argentina S.A.

Panamericana km 37,5
Centro Industrial Garín
Calle Haendel, Lote 3 (B1619 IEA)
Buenos Aires, Argentina

Livriz® de Docuprint
FÁBRICA DE BESTSELLERS